A BEST LIFE FINANCE WORKBOOK

PERMISSION TO SPEND

Diane Macias

www.BestLifeFinanceCoach.com

Print ISBN: 978-1-09834-956-1

eBook ISBN: 978-1-09834-957-8

TABLE OF CONTENTS

WELCOME!

You picked up this book for a reason. If you aren't sure this is the book you need, ask yourself these four questions:

1. *Do I know, or does my spouse/partner know, everything about our finances?*
2. *If something were to happen to me or my partner, or both of us, would someone else be able to take care of our financial affairs?*
3. *Am I free of any anxiety or stress revolving around my finances?*
4. *Am I living my best life?*

If you answered No to any of these, then read on!

HOW TO USE THIS BOOK

This book is a map, your map. It's your guide to getting your financial life planned and organized. This workbook will get you on the path to living your best life! For this, you'll need some supplies:

1. Keep a pen and highlighter on hand
2. Two 1.5-inch three-ring binders
3. A total of ten tab, three-ring dividers
4. A pad of sticky notes
5. Extra paper

This workbook will walk you through how to create financial stability in your life, and create two binders to organize your financial documents. These binders will be called the **Magical Budget Binder** and **Magical Future Binder.** Keep these together as a set.

Throughout this book there will be areas where you need to answer questions and gather information. *Do not skip ahead. Do not skip the steps. Do not skip the steps. Do not skip the steps.*

Wait, what? Skipping steps is ok? No. Do not skip the steps! Think about this in cooking terms. IfI make macaroni and cheese but without draining the water, I add in the cheese, technically, it is still food. You can even eat it, but *ugh. Who would want to?* Cooking out of order can quickly ruin a very easy dish. Like your finances, you can save and pay your bills, but are you watering down something that could be so much better? Yes. You are missing steps that could change your macaroni dinner into a gourmet meal. Now, I am not a natural cook, and I don't really enjoy it, but if I feed my family macaroni for dinner every night, no one will be happy. So, when I attempt to make something new, I have to follow the recipe. If I don't, it might be considered edible, but it could be mushy or burnt or too salty. The possibilities of lousy food are endless. If I don't follow the directions, I might have to throw it out and feed my family cereal. It's the same with your budget. By following these steps,you'll create a gourmet life. Set yourself up for success, and start with an open mind and a nice, clean budget that will be your recipe for success. Stop eating cereal thinking it's ok.

Read this book carefully, make notes in the margins, highlight, scribble, and put stars and circles on parts you want to remember. Take time and be thoughtful when filling in the answers to questions, and be thorough when entering financial information. No one will check your answers or make sure you did your work, but the truth is, by doing your part, you're taking your life in your hands, and you will be the one who benefits. And then reread it if you find you're losing your path or need reminding.

Some advice about getting your partner involved: If you're the person who primarily handles the finances in your home, ask your partner for some help getting a little more organized. Show them this workbook and tell them about the binders you'll create and ask them for help to fill it in. If your partner primarily handles the finances, tell them you found this book and ask if you can help in any way. Surveys have found that when asked, the person who is the primary financial caretaker of the household, almost always says yes when offered help. It's often a burden they would love to offload. Chances are, they would love your support if they have been shouldering the burden. If your partner is excited about making your dreams come true, then *yay!* Make a point to work together diligently in this workbook until it's complete. Make it an after-dinner activity or plan weekly sessions. However, if you have a partner who isn't so happy to make changes, go ahead and read this book anyway and highlight what stands out to you. Make changes and suggestions where you can. Once your partner sees positive changes begin to happen, they might be more open to working through this with you. This workbook can bring you financial peace of mind, and allow people who share finances to come together.

Part One of this book uncovers your emotions revolving around money. While we think about money in numbers, our emotions govern how we save or spend. The exercises will help you understand how money has played a part in your life, what you think about money, and how you handle it. Understanding how your emotions stand in your way of financial success is vital. I'll also talk about habits and mindsets that will help you stay on track with money going forward. You'll visualize the life you should be living. Dreaming is absolutely necessary for achieving your goals.

Part Two will help you gather information about your income and expenses. First, I'll help you create a detailed list of everything you spend. Then you'll need to consider savings, insurance, and retirement accounts. Knowing where you stand financially is a necessary step in the right direction.

Part Three will walk you through getting organized and creating your own **Magical Budget Binder,** where the "dreaded budget" becomes your road map to freedom. And **Magical Future Binder**, where you will keep your insurance, retirement documents, and will or trust. If you aren't already, this workbook is where you'll get yourself organized. These binders are crucial to whoever needs to handle your financial affairs when you cannot at any point in your life. Creating this gift for yourself and your loved ones is invaluable—treat them well and keep these files up to date and complete.

So that's it—three steps to financial freedom! You see, you were nervous for nothing!

As you read along, if you need more space to write out your answer at any time, use your blank paper and tuck it inside this book next to the question. Some questions will ask about your own experiences, hopes, and dreams. Other spots are for gathering information about your bills or your paycheck. All of this will help you get to the part where you learn how to create a personal budget. No one expects you to be an expert right out of the gate or even a few months down the line. This workbook will walk you through the process, bit by bit. Starting is the first step that you need to start living your best life!

"A journey of a thousand miles starts with a single step."
— Lao Tzu, Chinese proverb

INTRODUCTION

Hello, my name is Diane, and I am a saver. I was raised by two savers. As an adult, I am finding that this is a rare combination for couples. I married a spender, a free spirit. For the first time in my life, I had to deal with someone else's spending habits, and they were wildly different from my own. I had no idea what to do. Luckily, our incomes outpaced the spending, but when the company I worked for shut down while we were expecting a child, we had to make changes—immediately. We cut back on everything we could think of, and then, little by little, we cut back even more. We decided that since jobs were scarce in 2009,I would take this time to stay home and raise our little one until the economy turned around. I quickly realized that no matter what the economy did, I still wanted to stay home with our child.

However, even with the spending cutbacks, I was struggling to save money. I was always worried that we wouldn't have enough. Flashback to my childhood: When I was about eleven years old, my dad, an electrical engineer, lost his job. In my memory, it was because the Cold War ended, and whatever it was he was designing was no longer needed. What made a HUGE, lifelong lasting impression on me was that we lived off his savings for about a year—a family of five and two of us kids in private school. WhenI grew up and got my first job, I squirreled away as much as possible. I was laid off, not once, not twice, but three times. I lived off my savings the first two times. It was the third time when I was sharing the finances with my husband that my life changed. We viewed money completely differently. My husband thought that if he worked harder and earned more money, he could play now and pay later. This line of thinking stressed me out to no end.

At this point, I started tracking our monthly expenses. Tracking, not budgeting. Each month, I showed my husband how much money we spent and would tell him, "We need to save more!" Some months we did, and some months we didn't. I would worry every time the property taxes were due or when we had to buy gifts. I was a ball of nerves during every holiday season, and thinking about retirement sent me into a panic. I had no idea if we were saving enough. Most years we maxed out the 401(k), but there were years when stocks went down, down, down. There were times that we justified not maxing it out. We wanted to save for a house, or we were stretched a little thin. It yo-yoed. We thought we had time to make up for it. It turns out that we didn't, and it hurt us more than we could have imagined. For years, I tried to find out if we were saving enough, but I never got a straight answer or a plan to follow, even from financial advisors. Even taking a vacation stressed me out to no end. Taking the money out of the savings account for plane tickets and hotels was gut-wrenching!

Why? In my mind, we were robbing ourselves of the security that came with growing a nest egg. Worse than that, we could not agree on how to spend or save our money.

Then, I heard about a finance course for couples and signed up. My spender husband was not happy. He asked me why we were going to a finance class when I already knew what to do. That was the problem—I didn't know what I didn't know. In fact, ***I was one hundred percent positive that I didn't know everything I needed to know about how to handle our finances.*** As the years have gone on, I realized that this is everyone's problem. No one knows what they don't know. *Duh.* This stuff—this money stuff—could be manageable. Society has conditioned us to think that talking about money or salaries is rude, but that line of thinking has kept generations in the dark when it comes to their finances. Unless our parents taught us well, we struggle. Unnecessarily, we struggle.

That first class is where I learned how to budget. The dreaded budget of which everyone is afraid and people resist with all their might. What a game-changer! I learned that while there was room (a lot of room) for improvement, we were doing OK in some places. In the areas we weren't, we now had a plan to take care of it. Once we were taught, it wasn't hard. A few skills can change a person's life. Knowing this gave me so much peace of mind and a sense of security. Passion for financial success replaced our fear. I began to read everything I could on how to save and invest. Seriously, I read a lot. I read blogs and articles and books. So many books! I slowly made changes to the way we saved and spent our money. It was a process, one change at a time, and my husband and I got better at it as time went on. The "dreaded budget" changed our lives. It changed our future! It has the power to change yours, too.

Then, a crazy thing started happening. People were asking me to help them with their own finances. One day, my sister-in-law suggested that I start an online group to post the articles I'd read and forwarded to her, thinking it could help other people, too. I was apprehensive, but I didn't think it could hurt. The next thing I knew, I had a few hundred followers, and my group was growing. I wasn't getting a ton of interaction, but people who never commented or interacted online kept telling me in person how much an article or tip helped them. As a result of this positive feedback, I kept posting. Guess who started telling people to make a budget? My free-spirited husband! Now, he's the first one to encourage people to get on top of their finances. He says that his greatest fear was that we would take that financial class, and we suddenly wouldn't be able to have fun anymore. Having to limit the life you live is a common concern for many people who I talk to about their financial matters. People are afraid that they have to suffer or sacrifice to manage their money. In reality, what it did for us was enable us to spend without guilt or fear. We could take those vacations and not stress out about it! We could buy gifts, go out to dinner, and not cringe when we paid. For us, the permission to spend was true freedom. It turns out that the dreaded budget was the best thing that ever happened to us.

After I had the online forum for awhile, I began hosting the same two-month finance course that my husband and I had taken a few years earlier. Helping people get on top of their finances became my top priority, and I started buying and giving people finance books I liked. People started telling me about their situations, and I found that far too often, people were scared, just like I had been. They would say, "Oh, you don't even want to know what our finances look like!" or "I am clueless. My husband/wife/partner handles all of that." The most common comment was, "We tried a budget, and it didn't work." They were worried about mountains of credit card debt or never getting to the bottom of student loans. They feared they started too late to save enough for their retirements. Listen to this carefully—**It is never too late to make a difference in your future.** The earlier you start, the easier it can be, but ***do not let starting late derail you from starting at all.*** Your only enemy is procrastination, and you are one hundred percent in charge of that.

More and more people asked me to sit down with them and sort through their finances, and hearing their stories lit a fire in me. I wanted to help people, but I also felt like I needed some structure to help them, so I found a financial coaching course and signed up. Suddenly, everything was coming together, including the idea for this book. I wanted to take the system I had been using and create a step-by-step guide that anyone could follow without being overwhelmed.

You might be feeling anxious about making changes to how you save and spend. Maybe you're afraid you won't do it right. Perhaps you have an irregular income, so you think you can't budget. Let these fears go because you absolutely *will not* do it perfectly the first time, the second time, or maybe even the seventh time. It isn't about being perfect. A good process, even done imperfectly, will create positive changes. ***Think about the stress and anxiety in your life that is caused by financial uncertainty. This book will help you overcome that.*** Step by step, by filling in these pages, you will discover how you want to live your life and what it will take to get there financially. What money and financial awareness means to you will be different from someone else. For you, it could be saving to take a vacation of a lifetime, getting out of serious debt, or finally understanding what your actual financial situation is and making a plan to become financially independent. It might even be different from your partner, so this book will help you get on the same page or decide how to align and make all your goals a reality.

You have the power to make your goals and dreams come true. However, you can't do that if you don't know where you stand. A map is useless if you don't know where to start! Stop beating yourself up about mistakes or hardships you have with money. Once you fill in this book, you'll have a clear picture of where you are financially, and where you're heading. This book will be your map. You'll have filled in the holes and solved problems you might not have even known you had. Stress and anxiety caused by your finances will no longer nag at you or keep you up at night as you wonder about what you don't know is happening financially. *That's when you'll be able to live your best life!*

There is one more important consideration that you must think about. Besides improving your quality of life, there is also a very real, grave reason that everyone needs to understand very clearly when it comes to your money. Someday, you will die. When that day comes, whether it's at the end of a long, long life, or sneaks up out of nowhere, someone you love will have to deal with your finances. When that happens, will it be easy for them, or will they be hunting for information, possibly cursing you in the process? Whoever will deal with the reality of your departure should be able to pick up your **Magical Budget** and **Magical Future Binders** and take care of all of your bills and financial affairs. If you haven't settled your finances properly, the court—*not your family*—will decide who gets your money. This process will take months, even years, and cost many, many thousands of dollars. Your money and assets will be divided in whatever way a judge decides, making a difficult time even more difficult for your family. I've seen it happen so many times. Taking a bit of time now and filling in these pages will keep your family from financial heartache.

The great news is that by planning and preparing, you're setting yourself up for financial freedom! So what if you have an unexpected medical bill or your car needs new tires? You've got all that covered. Oh, and you or your partner loses a job? No sweat, you have a plan in place. And retirement? One hundred percent all over it! You're going to kick back in style. Maybe travel or buy a boat. Why not both? And you are teaching your kids to handle money before they start making mistakes. They'll start saving for retirement with every paycheck they ever get. They will learn to save and spend responsibly. You'll teach your kids exactly what they need to do to live the best life possible. ***Stress and anxiety that is caused by your finances will go away when you're in charge and know where you stand. And that's when you'll be able to live your best life!*** What you're doing right now is creating a legacy of success.

Wow! I am so impressed with you! You started here a little unsure, but now you've changed your family's lives for generations! Let that sink in a little.

Doesn't that feel great!

PART ONE: PRINCIPLES AND PURPOSE

WHERE YOU CAME FROM AND WHERE YOU ARE GOING

First and foremost, your money should keep you safe. You need money to pay for your home, food, transportation, and clothing. After that, what would you do if money was not an issue? Imagine you have all the money that you could ever want or need. What do you do with it? When you don't have to think about a job, what do you spend your time and energy doing? How does it impact your family, your community, and your legacy? Sure, if we had all the money we could hope for, we might all run out and buy houses and cars, and that's great, but after that, what would money do for you and others? After you have all the material objects you've wanted for yourself, what impact would you make on the world? For example, in the early 1990s, Rosa Parks, the prominent civil rights leader, was robbed and assaulted at the age of 81. A stranger to her, Mike Ilitch, the Little Caesars founder, heard the story, and like a fairy godmother, quietly got her an apartment in a safer neighborhood and paid her rent for ten years until she died. Wealth becomes the magic that we need to help people. Giving is the real power of money, not buying fancy cars.

The famous Prime Minister from the United Kingdom, Winston Churchill, said, "We make a living by what we get, but we make a life by what we give." When I sit down with people, I ask them what money can do for them and others. How can they change lives with money? So now I'm asking you, what is important about money to you? What dreams and fairy godmother acts do you have that require money?

Take a few minutes and write down all the reasons money is important to you—after all the necessities of life are taken care of, what dreams can you make come true? If you're in a relationship with someone who shares your finances, discuss these key points together. You might find that your ideas are vastly different, but that's the beauty of this exercise: Everyone's dreams can come true if you plan for it. Are you planning this future with someone, or are you on your own? Have your partner complete each of these questions as well.

What dreams do you have that require money?

____

____

____

____

____

Take a marker and put a star on that answer. And then write it down on sticky notes and post them where you will see them every day, taped inside your wallet, on your bathroom mirror, your computer monitor, and your bedside lamp. *Why money is important to you is why you're doing what you're doing.* It is why you are making changes. If you lose sight of that, you won't stick to the plan. It's OK if your plan changes, but don't abandon it because you've forgotten what it is.

And remember: Having money doesn't guarantee you an easy life. There are countless examples of celebrities and star athletes who earn large salaries, struggle financially, and eventually declare bankruptcy, losing millions of dollars. We might even think to ourselves, *how careless, how could they be so dumb!* Imagine if I gave you all the ingredients to make cookies but didn't give you a recipe. What are the odds that the cookies would turn out well? First, how much experience do you have baking? If you were an experienced baker, you might be able to pull something decent together, but most people's cookies wouldn't be stellar. It is the same with money, it isn't hard if you know what to do. Sadly, most of us have never been given the recipe for personal finance. If you are struggling, be kind to yourself. This book is going to help you learn the recipe. We'veall made mistakes with money. We either learn and move on or keep making them. Which will you do?

I like to ask new clients about how their parents handled money. My parents were savers, and following their example, I became a saver. Eating out was reserved for birthdays and big celebrations. Our vacations were to visit family or to go camping, and we rarely flew. I bring this up because most people will handle money the same way their parents did. Of course, there are always exceptions to this, and some will consciously make efforts to manage their finances differently, and they succeed. However, unless you educate yourself like you are right now, you might find yourself in the group of people who try to do the opposite of their parents but get the same result. For example, if your parents had low-income jobs and struggled to pay the bills or save, you might get a good-paying job but spend all your money, struggling the same way. I talked to a man whose father had made poor retirement investments and died, leaving his widow very little. In an attempt to not make the same mistake, this man saved a lot of money. Yet, he didn't invest any of it, putting himself in a similar situation for his retirement because he didn't take advantage of earning compound interest. Luckily, by getting some guidance and education, he made changes before it was too late. You see, even if your parents didn't sit you down and talk you through it, you learned to handle money from watching them.

So, what did your parents do with their money? Take a few minutes to think about this and write down how you grew up watching your parents deal with your home's finances. Did you grow up in a single-parent home, or did one parent handle everything? Did they make joint decisions? What worked for them? Where did they struggle? Did they agree on the finances, or did they fight about money? Do you have any idea how they handled their money?

How was money handled in your house growing up?

____

____

____

____

____

Now, think about what positive or negative statements your parents said about how **YOU** manage your money. Did someone tell you that you waste or lose money or are irresponsible with money? ***Are the words your parents used in your head? Do you believe them, or can you see now that these words don't define you?*** Just having the insight to this is valuable. Understanding why you do something is sometimes enough to bring about change.

What were you told about how you handle money? Was it positive or negative?

____

____

____

____

____

Teaching Your Kids

Having thought about financial lessons your parents taught you, either deliberately or by example, what lessons would you like to teach your kids or young people in your life? What would you tell them to do differently or similarly? What do you wish you had known earlier? And most importantly, now knowing what you were told about how **you** handle money, what will you say to your children about managing money? ***Once children can count, even on their fingers, they're old enough to start learning about finances.***

This includes teaching children to be responsible or irresponsible with money. ***Children are set up to fail when they are discouraged or kept from learning about financial responsibilities. Maybe this happened to you.***

When I was a young mother, I was a part of a Mothers of Preschoolers or MOPS group. Every meeting, we had a speaker. One day, when my child was three years old, our speaker told us to get three jars and label them "Spending," "Saving," and "Sharing." Spending was, of course, to use as you pleased. Saving was for a special or essential purchase down the road. And the sharing jar was to be spent on other people. She suggested we start giving our children monthly "commissions" to help with age-appropriate daily chores. The idea is that they care for and help keep the household in order because they lived there. We would give our child one dollar for every year old they were and explain to them that they could choose to put the money into whatever jar they wanted.

Being three years old and getting three dollars, the choice was simple—one dollar in each jar. As the years went on and the chores became more work-intensive, the commissions grew, and it was still up to my kid to put these extra dollars into whatever jar she wanted. When she was nine years old, I found out that she continued splitting the money evenly despite now knowing that she could only spend one-third of her money. We opened a bank account for her, and she had hundreds of dollars to deposit into the Saving category. I found out that inside her wallet, she had taped labels into the two pockets, "Spending" and "Sharing." On days that treats were sold at school, she used her Sharing money to buy her friends treats that hadn't brought money with them. I learned to save for giving as an adult; this little girl doesn't even know that isn't just what you do. ***Some of your money isn't yours. It's to help someone else.*** It is your fairy godmother money.

Later, I discussed these jars with friends, and we decided this concept should include a fourth jar: Investing. Shortly after that conversation, we talked to our daughter about the stock market and what it is. We showed her how to read a stock profit and loss graph and helped her buy stocks with her savings. David Bach, the author of Smart Couples Finish Rich, learned this same lesson from his grandmother at age seven. Imagine giving your children the confidence in knowing that investing is just another thing to do with money. There is no limit to how much you can teach your kids.

Another bit of wisdom came from a picture I came across online. The picture looks like a board game, but each square represents $25. To play the game, your child must save money, and with every $25 saved, color in a square. The game must be completed by the child's eighteenth birthday, having saved a total of $1000. This game is genius! It teaches kids to save, and before they're off to college, they have a thousand-dollar emergency fund! To further motivate my kid, I told her that I would match dollar for dollar any amount over $1000. So, if she saves $1500, I will give her an additional $500, giving her $2000 to start her emergency fund. Talk about motivation! You can find this game on page 141.

There is so much we can pass on to the next generation from what we learn. If you aren't sure about something, find out. Ask a professional, do an internet search for ideas, or chat with other people about what they're doing to teach their children about money. Letting your kids figure it out on their own isn't the answer, because like the rest of us, they don't know what they don't know. A little guidance can go a long way!

What financial wisdom would you like to teach the younger generation?

____

____

____

____

____

Evaluating Yourself

Now that you know what money means to you, it's critical to consider where you want to end up. Do you love your job, or do you dread walking into work? Do you like your neighborhood, or would you like to move? Are you able to pay your bills comfortably, or are you struggling? Is your life going the way you want it to go, or do you dream of a different life? What would you change? After all, you can't change your situation if you aren't entirely clear about what you want instead. Often in the busy-ness of life, we forget to plan, so take some time to imagine: where do you want to see yourself in a month, a year, five years, or ten? What goals do you have? What does the future look like for you? Saying, "I want to be rich" isn't the answer. At least not the full answer.

Wanting to live comfortably and have a secure financial future is a start. If you aren't where you want to be, let's change that! Where do you want to live? What does your house look like? Do you travel, or do yoga? How does your dream smell? Is it salty like the sea or fresh like mountains after rain? When you wrote out what money meant to you, what did you discover that tugs at your heartstrings? Would you like to teach orphans chess, or build with Habitat for Humanity, or create a rescue sanctuary for animals? What would fill up your heart now and in the retirement phase of your life?

You'll need to get some extra paper because visualizing your future in detail is critical. It's easy to get sidetracked. ***If you don't have a clear focus on what you want out of this life, it can slip into the forever of "someday."*** Don't let your dreams fade away because you didn't put a plan together. Life just happens to you when you don't plan for the best.

What is your ideal future life?

____

____

____

____

____

Wealth is the ability to fully experience life.
– Henry David Thoreau

What Are You Ignoring

Let's talk about what you're avoiding. Do you have medical debts or student loans or credit cards that you don't even want to *think* about paying? Are you spending more in a month than you make? Is your savings account empty? What's nagging at you? What is lurking at the back of your mind, keeping you from being at peace? Have you found yourself in a financial hole that wasn't your doing or in your control? As much as we wish these things would go away on their own, they won't. And if you don't deal with them head-on, they could get much worse. These not only weigh on you financially but keep you from really living. It's like a storm in the distance; you know it's coming, and it hangs over you like a black cloud waiting to rain. It keeps you from living your true and best life! Stop ignoring the storm and start preparing to withstand it. Write down everything that you know you need to take care of, and in **Part Two**, you're going to put together a plan to tackle it.

What do you need to deal with that you are ignoring?

What Can You Change

People can get stuck and have trouble imagining life being any different than it is right now. If you let go of the fear of change, you have the power to alter the course of your life. What shifts need to happen to make your dream-future a reality? Changes don't have to be all financial. Any positive transformations can make a difference. Don't leave any little bit out, even if it is waking up fifteen minutes earlier so you can have a better breakfast before work, or make a gratitude list at the end of each day so you go to bed happier. Of course, only you can decide what revisions you can make, but I am willing to bet the changes you make now are just the beginning. You are going to do great! Whenever you feel overwhelmed, take a deep breath and know that this situation can change for you.

What can you change about your situation?

SHARING FINANCES

Throughout this book, I'll be referring to couples working through their joint finances a lot. If you're single, I encourage you to find someone you trust to talk to about this process. Make sure it's someone who has your best interests at heart, not your retail therapy buddy, but ideally, someone who is on top of their finances, someone you know will be honest with you and help guide you. Ask them to be your Accountability Partner, the person you can call and talk through a big purchase or other financial decisions with. Throughout this book, when I suggest couples do an exercise together, single folks can work through it with an accountability partner and revisit it later if they become financially attached to someone.

What about if you aren't sure if or how to combine your finances with someone? Finances are a crucial topic in a relationship. Both of you must be completely transparent with your finances. Before moving in with or marrying someone, I suggest you run your credit reports and go over them together. Does this seem like an invasion of privacy? **If you or the person you are involved with are unwilling to take a detailed look at your credit reports together, then do not combine your finances.** Many advisors would tell you not to combine finances until you are legally married.

A Discussion

If you are thinking of combining finances with someone, discuss these questions in detail before you head off to the bank.

1. What is your credit score? (Run your credit reports and share!)
2. Do you tend to be a spender or a saver?
3. Do you have debts?
    a. If so, how much?
    b. What's the payoff plan?
4. How much money do you make?
5. Are you saving for retirement?
    a. How much do you have for retirement?
6. How much do you save each month?
7. How will we decide how to spend our money?

8. What is the most we can each spend before we discuss it with each other?
9. How should we split paying for the bills?
10. Will one person be the primary finance manager or will we do it together?
11. Should we get a pre-nup before getting married?

Checking Credit

Taking a good look at your credit report at least once a year is a good idea for everyone. The first time I ran my credit report was when I was buying my first house, and to my surprise, there was a small judgment on my credit report for an account that I thought had been closed, but due to an error, the last payment was unpaid. Sitting there, eating away at my good credit was a small blunder that could have quickly been taken care of years earlier. With identity theft on the rise, everyone needs to keep a close eye on their credit. Besides mistakes, there could legitimately be judgments or debts that you believe might make your honey have second thoughts about taking the next steps in becoming attached financially. Hiding these numbers will only make things worse down the line. Besides, if you have a low credit rating, and are honest about it, your person can help you get on top of it. If you hide it, and it comes out when you're trying to buy a car or house together, it could be a bigger problem between the two of you. It doesn't have to spell doom if you're upfront about it.

There are three credit bureaus: Experian, Transunion, and Equifax. Be aware that some companies do not report to all three, so there may be something on one credit report and not another. Checking your credit report can be very simple and should be free if you are checking your own. You might be required to enter a credit card for verification or create a login. Make sure that you cancel any subscriptions before the free or grace period ends for these services.

Here are the three websites: https://www.experian.com; https://www.transunion.com; https://www.equifax.com

What's your credit score? Were there any surprises?

____

____

____

What's your partner's credit score? Any surprises to you or them?

____

____

____

Systems For Sharing

There are three main ways to deal with finances with someone else:

1. **Separate but separate.** This setup is like having a roommate more than a partner. Each person pays half, or some predetermined amount for bills, out of their individual accounts, never getting a joint account in this scenario. This system keeps you separate in your spending habits, but it makes it very difficult, ifnot impossible, to come together for mutual goals. However, if you aren't married, this is a **practical and safe** way to safeguard your money, should you break up.

2. **Separate but together.** Similarly, couples would keep their individual accounts but also have one joint account. An agreed-upon amount would be put into the joint account each month to pay for all the bills and joint expenses such as housing costs, bills, food, and entertainment. The rest would stay in their personal accounts to do as they wish. Unless you're married, it's advisable to keep your finances separate. However, if you insist on having a joint account, then this system could work for you. Keep nomore than one month's expenses in this account should your relationship go sideways.

3. **Together forever.** Once you're legally married, this is the most transparent and easiest way to set up your finances. Deposit all paychecks and income directly into one joint account. All bills, groceries, gas, etc., and savings come out of this account. Each month, "fun" money will be transferred into each person's

separate individual account. Fun money pays for any hobbies, activities with friends, or even gifts for each other. This setup is most conducive for achieving joint goals, and if both people are upfront with their spending, is the easiest to track.

Examine your situation and decide what makes the most sense to you. I've read about variations and tweaks to these three systems, but they were so minor that it's best left between you and your partner to make any modifications that you see fit. Some married couples will choose to keep finances separate for various reasons, and that is OK—as long as you both agree and have a system that is transparent, makes sense, and protects you both.

What method will you and your partner use to combine your finances?

____

____

____

Will one person be the primary financial caretaker?

____

____

____

Do you both agree?

____

____

____

Planning Ahead

If you're already married or living with someone, how are you handling your joint expenses? Is it working for both of you? Do you have anxiety about what you are spending on the bills? I'm going to talk a lot about handling saving and spending in this workbook, so if you're not on the same page now, it's OK. This workbook will help you get through a lot of your challenges. ***Financial conflicts can destroy relationships, but working together can make dreams come true.***

I'm about to lay down some harsh realities. Take a deep breath; it's going to be ok. I'm writing to you as a stay-at-home mom, and although my husband brings in the majority of our income, I'm the financial caretaker of the family. I'm here to tell you that bringing in or not bringing in an income does not make it any more or less your business or your responsibility to manage the money that comes in or goes out of your home. Hear this clearly: ***You must find a way to be financially equal to your partner, and you must support your partner in having financial equality.***

Wow, did I just tell you what to do? Yes, I did. Due to earning lower wages and taking time off to raise children and caring for elderly parents, even full-time working women end up with substantially smaller retirement accounts. Whatever your income situation is, each person needs to have a fully funded retirement account and an independent income stream. Period.

In the years that I've been helping people, the number one reason people come to me is divorce.I could go into the statistics of separation and all that heartbreak, but we all know how devastating the dissolution of a marriage can be on finances, and we all know someone or have been that someone who has been through it. So, do yourself a favor and fully fund two retirement accounts. Easy peasy. And if you're still together at the end of your days, you'll have a bigger cushion for your retirement years. Staying in a bad marriage or relationship because you can't make it on your own financially is a tragic way to live. Statistics show that fewer and fewer couples are getting married these days, but that isn't stopping them from splitting up. Unfortunately, ***more than a third of single mothers are considered poor. Women are more likely to be alone at the end of life, either by choice, divorce, or death.***

Despite women living to nearly eighty years old, the average age of widowhood is sixty years old. Sadly, elderly, single women are the most likely to live in poverty. Whether you work full-time, part-time, or stay at home, put a plan in place to keep your independence intact in case life takes an unexpected turn. It only takes a little planning and forethought to avoid a possible disaster.

These are the decisions you and your partner should be able to make together. If opening the topic for discussion causes a problem, then there is a more significant issue at hand, and other professionals, like relationship counselors, should probably be involved. Partnerships should be equal, and if you find yourself in a relationship where finances are being withheld from one person, some things need to change. If this section is making you extremely uncomfortable, think about why. Is there something going on in your home that isn't sitting well with you? Work it out with your partner or therapist. If you're sharing finances, it's absolutely necessary to make a plan together that works for you both.

When you have peace and security within your finances, unnecessary stress and anxiety won't burden your relationship. You'll have the energy to make the life you want to live. By working together toward making your dreams come true, your relationship can become stronger than ever. We all know financial stress hurts relationships, but who knew that money could help it!

HABITS

As with any success, work needs to go into it. It doesn't have to be intense or even a lot of work, but it does need to be consistent and intentional. Like brushing your teeth, this little habit or lack of can make a huge difference in your health and smile. Even small habits will help you achieve financial success. The great benefit of financial independence, freedom, and security is that it spills over into the rest of your life. Leaving the stress and worry of money behind gives you the energy for your life's more critical pieces—your family, your friends, or your hobbies and passions. Being financially independent can keep you from a bad living situation, out of a toxic work environment, or burdening loved ones. The freedom that you'll have to live your life on your terms and achieve your dreams is worth every penny.

Live on Less than You Earn

When I say this to people, I get two reactions: The first is, "Well, duh! Why would you ever spend more than you earn?!" The second is, "That is impossible. I don't make enough to live on." To the people who fall into the first category, make sure that you're spending responsibly. Are you paying on cars and credit cards without a second thought? Can you really afford these payments, or are they keeping you from true financial freedom? In Part Two, you'll have a chance to check those numbers. For the people who are in the second category, this might be your situation right now. However, this isn't a sustainable lifestyle. You have two options: earn more or spend less. I suggest you do both. Immediately.

My favorite money guru, Warren Buffett, is famous for his words of wisdom. He says, "If you buy things you don't need today, you will have to sell things you need tomorrow." Warren Buffett is one of the wealthiest men globally. Marcus Tullius Cicero, a Roman statesman who lived over 2000 years ago said, "Frugality includes all the other virtues." And Robert Kiyosaki, Author of the book Rich Dad, Poor Dad has this to say, "It's not how much money you make, but how much money you keep, how hard it works for you, and how many generations you keep it for."

Take these words to heart. They can change your life.

When you think about your spending habits, do you tend to save or spend? Do you cringe when you have to pay for something or get a little rush from it? Did you identify with my husband or me? Are there times when you have spending or saving spurts?

Which type of money person are you, Spender or Saver? Are you sure?

Which type of money person is your partner?

If you have moments when you spend or save uncharacteristically, what brings that on? Stress or depression? Unexpected circumstances?

Pause Impulse and Extra Spending

As you go along, finding out where and how you spend money, I will teach you how to budget and plan, and your mindset will shift. A woman I know used to buy a coffee every time she went grocery shopping. She would walk right into the Starbucks, get an almond milk vanilla latte, and leisurely shop. There were two problems with this: she was spending close to $6 just walking in the door. And she would wander down the aisles slowly, with her latte in hand, casually browsing up and down, picking up more than she ever could need off the shelves and putting items into the cart. She started saving HUNDREDS of dollars in groceries every month by not getting that six-dollar latte. True story. Now, if it isn't on her grocery list, it has to have a good reason for going home with her.

How much do you think you spent on your indulgences last month? (Coffee, non-essential or mindless shopping, hobbies, etc.)

Total $__________

Of course, this goes for large items and small subscriptions alike. Cars, boats, dogs, the "it's only $2.99 a month" whatever app—have you researched it? Have you saved for it? Can you actually afford it?I put dogs on the list for a reason. While animals can make our lives quite fulfilling, they're costly to take care of and feed. If you're struggling to pay the bills, please wait to get a pet. It could be the motivation you need to get you to financial freedom faster! Now, there are two things I want you to remember when you want or "neeeeeeeed" something:

1. ***We nickel-and-dime our way into poverty.***
2. ***Just because you can pay for it doesn't mean you can afford it.***

A term I came across in my financial studies is **Secondary Poverty.** It was coined in England in the early 1900's by an English sociological researcher named Benjamin Seebohm Rowntree. It means that ***people are keeping themselves living below the poverty line, even though they earn enough to be above it, because they're spending money on non-necessities—things other than food, clothing, and a roof over their head.*** Mainly, he was talking about tobacco and gambling. What habits do you have that are keeping you from living the life you say you want? Are you buying lunch or coffee or snacks instead of bringing lunch from home? Are you wasting food by not paying attention to the expiration date or grocery shopping without a plan? Are you paying for more cell phone service than you need? What expenses are holding you back? How many streaming services do you have? Take an inventory of your non-essential bills. Is it really necessary to have three or four different streaming services? Cut back to one (or even zero while you tackle debt) and kick your goals into high gear! Remember, cutting back doesn't mean that you're never going to have any fun ever again. It's just the opposite. Some short-term sacrifices for long-term gain is worth it for six months or a year if it means that the rest of your life is on track.

List all monthly subscriptions and cost (non-utility) you have each month:

____

____

____

____

____

What do I mean when I say, "Just because you can pay for it doesn't mean you can afford it"? Isn't the very definition of having the money mean that you can afford it? The short answer is no. The longer answer is more of another question: ***Does this car payment/music service/shopping therapy, etc. help or hurt me on my path to my goals and dreams?*** If you sold the car that still has a $25,000 loan balance and bought a $5,000 car with cash, how fast would the extra $20,000 get you to your goal?

For years and years, my husband and I saved for a down payment for a house. The problem was, we couldn't save fast enough to outpace the housing market in San Diego, California. We just couldn't—there was no way! And by no way, I mean, we hadn't thought of a way. So, when we took our first finance class, and we saw that our car payments were killing, *KILLING,* our dreams, even though we could pay for them, and also had money left over to save, it became clear that we weren't doing nearly enough to get the job done. And to add insult to injury, when I looked up the Kelly Blue Book value of our cars, they were worth less than we owed. My car was three years old, had low miles, and nearly worth half of its price. Learning this changed *everything*. It turns out that ***new cars will lose 20-30% of their value in the first year! And by the fifth year, it will only be worth about 40% of the sticker price. Ouch.*** We cut back even more spending—we paid the cars off super fast and vowed never to buy new or have car payments again. Our savings, net worth, retirement, and dreams got a super boost, and we haven't looked back.

Take this time to make some rules or guidelines for yourself. I used to meet my friends out for lunch and dinner to socialize and catch up. Getting out of cooking is worth every penny to me, but I realized how much it slowed me down from reaching my goals. So, instead of a $15-$30 meal, I started meeting my friends for coffee. For $7, I could even get a muffin. I didn't tell my friends that I was cutting back on spending. I would just ask them to meet for coffee. Then, I started inviting people to my house! While cooking is no fun for me, I love to bake. So as to not eat all the baked goods myself, I would say, "Come over! I have coffee and cookies!" And I would even send them home with a few extras. Do you think anyone complained? Sure, I still go out for a meal on occasion, but it's now well within my plan, and it is no longer keeping me from my financial goals.

> *"...we justify our poverty and nickel-and-dime ourselves so far into debt that wealth is unattainable..."* — Claude La Vertu

So, what guidelines can you put in place to help you? Maybe buy a bottle of wine to enjoy at home with friends instead of meeting at a bar. Maybe buy yourself a pour-over coffee maker and start making coffee at home. A common indulgence is eating lunch out with co-workers. Perhaps you have a similar habit. One client started with one small change at a time. First, she started to buy a case of soda at Costco instead of buying a drink at lunch. That saved a few dollars a day, and as the savings increased, she cut back even more. She started only eating out on Fridays. Another client noticed that when she'd go shopping for gifts or household items, she'd pick up extra things from end caps and displays, but when she shopped online, she didn't fall for those impulse buys. Of course, this isn't the case with everyone! Know yourself. Where can you reduce your spending and make some rules for yourself? Write them down! Make a list of what you can cut and watch your goals become your reality.

What are you willing to do to minimize overspending?

____

____

____

What's your spending weakness?

____

____

____

Set It and Forget It — Sort of

Once you get your budget written down in **Part Two**, you'll see how much money you can save and find out if you need to save more. Once you have this information, I'll go over how you can put everything on autopilot, by removing the temptation to spend your savings and simplifying your life. Often, people save the money that is leftover at the end of the month. What's left usually isn't enough, and never as much as you could save by planning for it.

Bills: You may or may not have your bills paid automatically right now. *Automatic payments can save you lots of time.* However, you need to make sure that you don't overdraw your checking account. Once you've figured out how much money you need to pay for your daily expenses and monthly bills, this can be set up easily with your online banking. I like to have all my bills that don't fluctuate paid automatically. Even utility bills that are about the same every month can be paid automatically by setting up payments online. Most bills will have an option to pull payments from your bank account on or before the due date. Alternatively, you can set up automatic payments from your bank account to pay your bills. Initially, set up a schedule of when payments were due to be sure you have enough in your checking account. As time goes on, and you have more cushion in the budget and are more comfortable with this process, you should be able to let down your guard a little. This leads me to my next point.

Balances: Chances are, your bank can send daily account balances by text or email. Make a mental note and delete it. It takes three seconds. This habit will keep your account balance at the front of your mind. By checking your account balance every morning, you can catch overcharges and avoid overdrawing on your account. Then, when you check your bill schedule, you can be sure you have enough to cover the due bills. It isn't difficult, and it will save you time and money. ***Know what your checking account balance is every morning.***

401(k): Are you maxing out the 401(k) offered at your job? Can you afford to max it out now? If not, look at increasing your contribution from your paycheck by one percent every few months. The decrease in pay should be manageable by then because you'll handle your money more efficiently, and if it's still out of your reach, find ways to boost your income. If your job doesn't offer a 401(k), there are other options out there. Remember, you're the one who has to pay for your life after retirement. Don't let excuses now keep you living poorly later.

Make a list of all the bills you can have paid automatically, and set this up.

Have your bank send your checking account balance to you every day.

How much will you auto-transfer into your savings account each month? $_________

What are you contributing to your 401(k) each month? $_________

If it isn't the max amount, find out how you can increase contributions.

____

____

____

____

____

Monthly Budget Meetings

I can't stress how monthly budget meetings can make all the difference in the world. I am going to walk you through budgeting in **Part Two**. ***Review your budget every single month, not every other month or some months. Every single month, print out your budget, fill in what you spent, and review it with your spouse, partner, or accountability partner.*** Did you stick to your budget? Are you constantly going over budget in some areas? As the saying goes, are you robbing Peter to pay Paul, taking out of one account to pay for something you went over in another?A budget isn't set in stone, but make a conscious decision to change it as needed; don't let it go if you consistently go over budget. Make adjustments to the upcoming month's budget. If there is an event you need to account for or a large bill, plan for it. As the months and years go on, you'll get better at this. Your budget will be more accurate, and your anxiety will lessen, as long as you consistently review it.

Before I took my first finance course, I *thought* I was budgeting. All I was actually doing was accounting for my money as it left our accounts. I thought we should be able to save more. We were just spending too much. But without a plan, it is like going on a trip without knowing where you are going. You end up in a strange town, looking for a place to stay, wondering what you should see or do. Sure, you might find a hotel, but you end up paying a higher price than necessary for the last-minute booking. Does this town even interest you? Are you missing something amazing right under your nose because you didn't do your research? You could wing it and see how well it turns out, but if I am going to be spending hard-earned money on a trip, I want to make sure it is someplace I want to go. I want an itinerary and tours. I want the best trip possible. This is why you need a budget. Plan for the best possible outcome for your life.

Do not leave it to chance. Your budget is your plan. Plans can and will change, but a plan works out in your favor more often than not. ***Your life is the most incredible trip you can plan. Winging it will only get you so far.*** The last thing you want to have happen is to wake up at sixty-five years old and not have a plan in place to retire comfortably.

Seven out of ten couples don't budget consistently, AND nearly 70% of Americans cannot cover an emergency of $400-$1000, do you think that this is a coincidence? So, have your monthly budget meeting every month. EVERY MONTH. And there is a very practical reason why. If you are double-charged or miss a payment, you want to know right away. If you try to dispute a charge or late payment that happened six months prior, you might not be reimbursed, and chances are, you won't even remember that you didn't make that charge. You will keep more of your money in your hands if you check your statements every month. When you monitor your spending, you'll be more mindful, and you won't be as likely to overspend.

Most months will look pretty similar with small tweaks. Have your meeting close to the beginning of the month and make it an event. Have coffee, get some cookies, and set up on the porch or somewhere you can relax. In the beginning, this could take some time. Like with most tasks, the more you do it, the better you get, the less time it will take, and the more impressive your outcome becomes. Remember, this will take time to get right, so don't give up. Give yourself this gift.

Schedule your first Monthly Budget Meeting

Reoccurring on the_________th day of every month.

Be Reliable and Accountable

Think about what it is like when you are waiting for someone who is never late. You might be worried about them and be relieved when they come around the corner even twenty minutes late. But if they are always late, you might be annoyed instead of worried. Which person do you want to be? When you are running late, do you want the people waiting for you to be concerned or annoyed? When you respect a person's time and energy, they are more likely to respect yours. A reliable person will be the first in line for those raises and promotions. When you are on time for work, dressed for success, people will notice you with a smile on your face. They will also see if you are grumpy and complaining. At times, we all complain but catch yourself when you do. Don't let it become who you are. Don't be known as the complainer. ***Complainers do not win in life.***

Why in the world am I telling you to smile and be on time? That comes to our next topic and probably what determines success more than anything else. Your mindset.

MINDSET

No More Excuses — Your Brain Believes You

The Japanese have a word-kototama. It means "word spirit." Meaning, if you say it out loud, it brings it to life. Practically every culture has a similar idea. In the United States, people often say, "knock on wood," as if that will keep evil thoughts from taking form. "What you think about, you bring about" or "dress for the job you want" or "fake it till you make it." This is good advice! Great advice, in fact. It turns out that ***your brain believes what you tell it***, not the other way around. Your mind is processing details of our lives at an incredible level. It makes decisions based on observations and information subconsciously. ***By having negative thoughts about money, you are telling your brain to stay away from money!*** You begin making decisions subconsciously that keep you from making or keeping money! Words and ideas are powerful. Of course, not all good thoughts can fend off all ill fates, but there is something so powerful about our beliefs that humans in every culture and time have used wishful thinking, prayers, and mantras to bring good fortune into our lives. Remember to use your words and thoughts wisely.

Before I started being mindful of my own money, I used to see fancy cars and designer bags and think, *what a waste of money!* I would think about what I would do with all that cash if this *moron* hadn't squandered it away on something that loses value every second. Even I had negative thoughts about money. (And I now know that some bags actually INCREASE in value!) Think about how often we hear how money is the root of all evil, or how the rich are selfish and greedy. Let's make one thing very clear: money is a tool, just like a hammer is a tool. You can build a house with a hammer or smash windows. You can use the money and help people in meaningful, life changing ways, or you can sit back with your piles of money and do nothing extraordinary. Money does not have an agenda or a conscience or take any actions on its own. So, leave all negative thoughts of money behind. Now, when I see a fancy car, I think, "Good for them! They must have reached financial success to be able to afford that car!" I don't know if they made a wise decision or not, but my own financial success depends on me and my thoughts.

Do you doubt this line of thinking? As my finance hero, Warren Buffett, said, "I never doubted for a moment that I wouldn't be rich." Your brain will do whatever you train it to do. I even read that your immune system gets a boost when you dress up and look your best. Your brain thinks, "Oh, here I am looking good; I must feel good, too!" So, banish all negative thoughts about money! ***Think positive thoughts about your future, your finances, your ability to create the world you want to live in, and watch the changes happen.***

Our country is in a financial crisis, but you do not have to be one of the masses. You can change your thoughts and change your life. Think about how much you are going to be able to do, and save. Think about showing what success looks like to your kids and grandkids. Think about how easy you are making your family's life after you leave this world. Think about your dreams coming true. You can do this and a whole lot more! Kick all negative thoughts to the curb. When you catch yourself thinking or saying something that has no value, rethink it, and re-say it. Your brain will believe you!

Hate Debt

Really, is that necessary? Yes. Debt will keep you from your goals. All debt. There is no "good debt." I hear people all the time saying that their student loans or mortgage is good debt. School, home, and car debts should be as temporary as possible. Imagine your student loans have only a 3% interest rate, but you are paying $500 a month. What could you be doing with that money? How much faster would you fund your retirement account? How much quicker could you save for a house? And what about that mortgage! Housing is usually the largest line item on a budget. Is it possible to buy a home with cash? Yes. Is that realistic for most of us? No. Think how much your mortgage or rent is every month. Now, how much less money would you need to live on if you didn't have to pay for the biggest housing expense. Generally, rents will increase every year and the tax break from that mortgage payment isn't a reason to keep paying it forever. When you pay off your mortgage, you'll probably have to pay a few thousand dollars in taxes each year, but you could be saving **hundreds of thousands of dollars** in interest payments to your mortgage company if you pay your mortgage off early. The math is very simple — pay less mortgage interest, and you will come out ahead.

Another argument for keeping mortgage debt is that you could be investing and make a higher return for your money. Dave Ramsey is famous for saying, ***"Personal finance is about 80% behavior. It is only about 20% head knowledge."*** So, will you take the money and invest it *well enough* to make up the difference in interest payments, or will that money get flitted away in the days of your life? We put our 401(k) contributions on hold to save for a house, but we didn't keep that money. At least not enough of it. We were careless with the extra money we had, and it put a massive dent in our retirement. Will investing money vs. paying off your mortgage increase or decrease your anxiety around your finances? Alternatively, how would you feel living in a paid-off home? How much extra cash will you have when your home expenses are only maintenance and property taxes? How much less money will you need if you don't have a house payment in your retirement years?

Some people borrow money for investment strategies. Borrowing for investments isn't something you should try if you have outstanding debts or insufficient emergency savings. If you are struggling with your finances, do not attempt to borrow money for investing. It is risky and requires a large safety net should the investment go sideways.

Chances are, you have some form of debt, and you'll probably need to take out a loan to buy a home, and that is ok, but we don't have to like it. If you resign yourself to it, ***debt will strangle you.*** If you hate it, you will get rid of it faster, and before anything else! Hate debt and see what positive changes your life will take on.

List your significant debts, like mortgages, school loans, and car loans?

___

___

___

___

___

Every time you borrow money, you're robbing your future self.
— Nathan W. Morris

Credit card debt is the worst kind of debt. You buy something you don't have the money for now and then pay 15-25% more for it month after month. Have you ever thought about how much that $5 coffee costs you after it takes you six months to pay off? If you don't pay off the entire balance on your credit card every single month, that is precisely what you are doing. And, it isn't just the interest that you are paying. Studies show that people buy 12-18% MORE when using credit cards versus cash. When I was about nineteen years old, I had a joint credit card with my family. My card had about a $150 balance on it. For some reason, my dad had to close the card, and he told me he would pay it off that one time. I felt so badly that he had done that, that I never carried a credit card balance again. I learned very early to pay with my debit card and to watch my balances very carefully. This lesson wasn't taught in school, or even deliberately by my dad. I just happened to feel ashamed about that incident that I changed my behavior. Most people have never been taught how to handle their finances. It is all by trial and error. How is that working out for everyone? Not great.

Headlines during the great government shutdown from December 2018 to January 2019 prove it. The US government was closed for thirty-five days, and around 800,000 people didn't get paid for close to two months. We know that about 70% of Americans can cover less than a $1000 emergency, which left about 560,000 people in a bad situation. Many went to food banks and used crowd sourcing to cover expenses. A little planning could have prevented this unfortunate situation for most of them. We don't even know what the worldwide financial implications of the COVID-19 pandemic are yet. The United States is experiencing job loss that hasn't been this high since the Great Depression. During this time, it isn't uncommon to hear people say, "We are all in the same storm but not in the same boat." Some families will be devastated by prolonged job loss or, worse, death. Don't leave the condition of your boat to chance. Plan ahead. Be prepared. Make sure that your boat can withstand the harshest storms.

If either of these or similar situations have affected you negatively, don't despair. You are learning here. I will talk about making a plan to get rid of any debt you have and what you can do to avoid getting any new debt. From now on, do not take on any debt aside from a mortgage. Keep even student loans and car loans to the bare minimum. Your goal is to buy everything with cash—yes, even cars—and ideally, your home. People do it, and you can too. Keep in mind how my zero-percent car payment effectively kept us from buying a house. So, that fifty-inch TV or cozy new couch that is zero percent for six months, if you have to buy it, buy it in cash. Jay Z is an American rapper who has grown his net worth to 900 million by being a shrewd businessman. His advice is, "If you can't buy it twice, you can't afford it." Do not fool yourself into thinking you are getting a deal with zero-percent *whatevers*. Remember, "the borrower is a slave to the lender" (Proverbs 22:7). The truth is that when you have to pay someone else, you are unable to pay yourself, and THAT keeps you from being someone's fairy godmother. ***DEBT is what keeps you from building real wealth.***

Forgive Yourself For Past Mistakes

Whew, this is a big one. I initially meant regarding your money, but as I sit here, I want you to do just that. Forgive yourself for your past mistakes. We wouldn't be human if we didn't mess up something here and there. Lessons will repeat until learned. And our decisions with money are no different. My husband and I bought brand new cars one year apart. Ugh. The total car payments due each month were mind boggling! Putting our 401(k) on hold to save for a house is another. You can forgive yourself because you are reading this book and doing all the steps, learning, and making a difference in your future. So, that brand new phone you bought, didn't insure, and dropped in the lake—let it go! When you put your savings on a hot stock tip that you heard at the gym and lost it all, let it go! Oh, and that time you didn't start saving for your retirement until you were almost fifty, let it go! All of these mistakes are just momentary setbacks. Chin up, and put one foot in front of the other!

Which money mistakes will you forgive?

____

____

____

____

____

Let no feeling of discouragement prey upon you, and in the endyou are sure to succeed. — Abraham Lincoln

Hang Out With High Caliber People

Lastly, surround yourself with winners! Again, the great and wise, Warren Buffett, said this when asked what advice he would give a young person to become successful, "Whatever stage of life you are in, it's better to hang out with people better than you. Pick out associates whose behavior is better than yours, and you'll drift in that direction." Of course you will! Like attracts like. Learn from people who have done what you want to do! Read everything. Be curious. Never stop learning. Raise your vibration! You cannot fool the universe.

The list here is only a start. I just read that making your bed every morning sets up your mind to complete more tasks each day, so add making the bed to this list. There are many great books about what habits help you be successful and happy, so don't stop here. Get going!

List some new habits you want to start:

INVOLVING YOUR KIDS

If you have kids, they are probably noticing changes. Get them involved! Have them sit down with you during your budget meetings or summarize what you talked about afterward. Tell them why you are making changes and ask them if they have any ideas to help. If you have teens, have them figure out how much money they will need once they leave the house. They can look up rent prices, create a personal budget, and know how much money they will need to get started and keep going each month. Encourage part-time jobs and investing. If your children are young, print out the "Kids $1000 Emergency Fund" Game Board located in the back of this book. Copy as many as you need. Walk your kids through the game. Help them figure out how many years they have to save and how much they will need to put away each month to reach that goal. Teaching your kids how to save and plan before they leave home sets them up for success! Go, you!

By changing your mindset and teaching your kids how to handle money before they find themselves in debt or struggling, you are changing the lives of your grandkids and your great-grandkids! Just imagine for a minute what life opportunities you are creating for generations! Improving your financial situation isn't about how much money you make; it's about what you know, how you use that knowledge, and how much drive and determination you have to do it! No one is stopping you, and by finishing this book and making your binders, you are well on your way to living your best life!

PART TWO: GETTING TO WORK

THE BUDGET

How do you feel dreaming about your future? Excited? Optimistic? I hope so, because I am doing this to bring you hope and help your dreams become your reality. I realize that it might feel daunting or overwhelming for some of you, or feel entirely out of reach, so I encourage you to take a deep breath and know that you won't be figuring it out all in one day or on your own. Keep reading and go one step at a time.

So, why do you really need a budget anyway? I mean, as long as you have money in the bank, what's the big deal? Let's go back to cooking. I can tell you that I do not have the ingredients to make a six-course gourmet meal at any given time. I'd need to plan it and go out and buy the ingredients. But, chances are,I probably have spaghetti and some sort of bread and a side of some vegetables, perhaps carrot sticks or broccoli. It's not the most exciting dinner, but it's dinner, and it will get the job done. But the only way I can start this meal is by looking in the cupboards and finding out what I have to begin with. And that is how you start your budget—by finding out what you have, what income and expenses you have to start cooking. Now, would you be OK eating spaghetti every day? Me neither. If you want a six-course meal life, you have to plan for it.

Years ago, I started kung fu lessons. I was so intimidated by the people in there with their uniforms and their colorful belts. As a newbie, I got a plain belt, and as I learned the very basics, I got one stripe added until I had three lines. At that point, I had the basic skills to learn an actual form and start testing for my own colorful belts. I thought I would only continue until it became too hard. I am telling you this because, as I learned, I got better, and the next form was only a tiny bit harder than the one I learned before. It never got "too hard" because I got better as I went along. I am currently training for my black belt because I never stopped. If you don't stop or give up, you can do pretty much anything you want. That means that whatever reservations you have about making a budget, sticking to a budget, planning for, or saving enough for retirement, throw them out the window! One foot in front of the other until you get there. If I can do kung fu, you can budget!

The Numbers: Incoming

First, write down all of your income. Add up your take-home pay, that is the actual dollar amount that goes into your bank each month. If you are guaranteed a bonus, make a note of that. Do you pet sit or tutor? Whatever income you get right now, write it down. What happens if you do not get a regular paycheck? People who have irregular paychecks can absolutely use a budget. If you are in this boat, a side hustle to boost extra savings will be a must for your peace of mind. In the next section, I will walk you through calculating your monthly expenses, and it will help you determine if you are making enough. For this exercise, people with irregular incomes need the last six to twelve months of paystubs. If you don't have pay stubs, you can look up the deposits made into your bank, or ask your employer for a printout. Write down what you were paid each month. Take a look at your average pay per month. Is it about the same or all over the map? Could you pay all of your bills using the lowest amount as your base, or will the average pay cover your monthly expenses? Make a note on what number you decide to use as your "base" monthly income and why.

How much money do you bring home each month?

Monthly Paychecks	$________	*monthly*
Side Hustle	$________	*monthly*
Other income	$________	*monthly*
Other income	$________	*monthly*
Total income	**$________**	***monthly***

Take a look at these numbers. Do you only have one number? Getting additional income is a significant consideration moving forward. Never rely on a single source of income, so if you only have one paycheck coming in, start brainstorming and asking everyone what they have as a side hustle. Think about what hobbies or talents you have that you can turn into a part-time job. Make this a priority because if you suddenly lose your job, you don't want to rely solely on your savings. A side hustle or additional form of income can buy you much needed time in a job loss event.

Next, you will figure out what you make hourly. Even if you are salaried, I want you to calculate what you make per hour. Knowing your hourly wage can help you from frivolously spending your money. For example, your friends have invited you out to eat or shop. Look at everything in terms of how many hours you need to work to pay for it. Is it worth working for several hours for one meal out or a new outfit?

To calculate your take-home hourly wage, start with your total monthly take-home pay per job, and divide it by how many hours you work at that job each month. Remember, even if you are paid hourly, your take-home pay can be considerably less once you pay taxes, social security, retirement, and healthcare. How much money do you get to keep?

How much money do you make hourly?

(dollar amount earned per month / divided by hours worked per month = hourly wage)

Paycheck	$________	*hourly*
Side Hustle	$________	*hourly*
Other income	$________	*hourly*
Other income	$________	*hourly*

How do you feel about these numbers? Good? Not so good? Do you see that your efforts might be better focused somewhere else? Go ahead and jot down some notes and thoughts on this. Is it time to ask for a raise? Would your lazy Sundays be better spent developing your side hustle or other sources of income?

BRAINSTORM: What creative ideas can I think of that might maximize or increase my income?

____

____

____

____

____

The second source of income might not be or seem to be a big deal right now, and maybe you don't have any clear ideas on how to increase your revenue, that is OK! Right now, you are brainstorming and gathering data.

Keep these ideas at the forefront of your mind and start focusing on what you need to get going. Once you put the plan to work, it may need tweaking, but don't give up.

The Numbers: Outgoing

Before you go on, let's play a game. Guess what your total expenses are. Everything from housing and utilities down to Friday night happy hour. What do you think the total is that goes out of your bank account each month? If you have no idea, it's OK. That is what we are here to find out. Go ahead and make a wild guess anyway.

How much money do you think leaves your account every month? $__________monthly

Now, let's capture your expenses. To help you, I have created a list of the most common expenses to jog your memory. You will want to fill this in as **completely and as accurately** as possible, but do not put this off because you think the task is too big or seems impossible.

Remember, one step in front of the other, and keep going. You might need to add additional lines. Be sure to calculate how much you spend on gas and groceries, down to whatever $4.99 monthly charges you might have stacked up. All of them. Compiling all of your monthly expenses is going to be the most challenging part, and guess what, it isn't that hard! It could take several months to fine tune, and most people don't fully capture all of their expenses at first. There is always something due in six months that you forgot about or household items that you buy as needed and have no idea what it costs. It's OK. You will adjust the list when it comes up. Just doing a budget, even a slightly flawed one, will get you in a better place. As time goes on, the data you collect monthly will help make your budget more accurate. Print out the last several months' bank and credit card statements to help with this task. Mark them off as you add them to your list. Find the Common Monthly Expenses Worksheet in the Index on page 126.

Complete it as thoroughly as you can and put your total below.

What are your total monthly expenses? $__________monthly

How does it compare to your estimate?

If you are short on covering your expenses, how much more do you need? $__________monthly

What can you cut out or cut down on right now?

____

____

____

____

____

As you look at your monthly expenses, were you way off, or were you pretty close to your guess? How do you feel about that? Let that feeling sit with you for a minute. Use it to motivate you to answer the next few questions. You are on your way to getting a stronger hold on your finances. Are you already seeing expenses you can cut down or cut out? Look at some of your categories. Are you comfortable with how many hours of work your cable/streaming service is costing you? Chances are, you can trim down these expenses and boost savings and retirement funds. Is your income more than your expenses? Are your expenses more than your income? If they are, did you know that? Does that worry you? If you are just finding that out, pause. Don't panic! Take a good look at your list—are there places you can cut back? Circle line items that could be lowered or eliminated.

Remember, nothing is permanent. Your situation can change. And the changes you make can change. Short-term sacrifices can do wonders for boosting savings and retirement funds. One step at a time, keep going! If you find out that you need more income or a second income, go back a few pages where you started brainstorming how you could increase your revenue. How much do you need to bring in every month to start living your best life? Even if you are making enough to get by, you will have greater success weathering a bad storm if you have more than one lifeboat.

Pro finance tip: Before you spend your money on something new, whether it be a new pet, kung fu or guitar lessons, or anything else, find a side hustle to pay for it. Maybe it's dog walking or tutoring. Perhaps it is something more high-tech. Talk to everyone you know who has a side hustle. The internet and libraries have answers you may need! If you are thinking of adding another line to your budget, find a way to make the money for another payment. To get ahead, you have to be willing to do something more than you are doing now. You are in charge of your future. Take it by the horns!

Who can you talk to about their side hustle?

____

____

____

____

____

"I'm working full time on my job and part time on my fortune."
– Jim Rohn

DEBT

Lastly, let's review your debt. I talked about this extensively in the Habits section, and the chances are that you have some form of debt, and that is OK. For most of us, taking on debt is a part of life. Cars, college, and homes are all big-ticket items, and chances are, you will need a loan. And as you get organized, with time, even these can be paid for in cash. Can you imagine that? However, credit cards should never pay for lattes, gifts, or vacations. When you borrow money to buy things, whether it is 25% or 0% interest rates, it keeps you from building up your wealth. Keep this in mind as you continue. Whenever possible, save and pay cash for all purchases, big and small. To get a handle on your debt, you need to know how much you have. Student loans, credit cards, car loans, personal loans—find the total of all the balances of all loans other than a mortgage. If you own your home, we will look at that balance later.

How much non-mortgage debt do you have?

Bill	Total Balance	Monthly Payment	Interest Rate
Credit card			
Credit card			
Credit card			
Student Loan			
Car Loan			

Total Balance $________

Total Monthly Payments $________

Did you know that was how much you owed? Were there enough lines there for you, or did you need to add extra? What does that number do to your overall level of stress? These numbers bring us to the most significant reason everyone needs to budget.

PEACE OF MIND

Like I was panicking over the savings account that, in reality, was sufficient and the retirement account, which needed attention, you'll feel better knowing what you have and where you need to focus. Knowledge is power. Knowing these numbers can only help you. Take a minute to write down how you feel looking at these numbers, maybe for the first time, and how you'll feel when you aren't wondering or worried about having enough to pay for an emergency or retire comfortably. I will talk to you about how to tackle your debts in **Part Three**. Are you already having insights into what you need to do about it?

How do you feel looking at your expenses and debts?

How will you feel when you are debt-free?

SAVINGS

On to our next topic: Savings. Aside from steering clear of taking on debt, the next step is to beef up your savings as quickly as possible. Imagine that you had an unexpected trip to the ER or you owe this year in taxes, or like in my case, your boss told you that your department was laid off. How do you think you might feel? What if you have enough money in your bank to cover all of that? You just turned an emergency into an inconvenience. How would you feel then? Probably relieved, at the very least.

What is the first payment you would worry about being able to pay if you lost your job?

____

____

____

The first time I was laid off, I didn't even look for a job right away. I had been working like crazy for a start-up company that didn't quite make it off the ground. I was burned out and weighing my options. During my hiatus, I was shopping for art supplies. The manager of the store was an acquaintance. He talked me into applying for a job there since I could get art supplies 50% off. I told him I didn't want to work more than fifteen hours a week.

For several months, I lived a pretty chill existence. When I finally figured out what I wanted to do,I still had enough money to move across the country and join another company. What I loved about this time of my life was how much fun I had with my friends. My cost of living was manageable, and the income I had from the art store kept me from depleting my savings, and having savings didn't happen by accident. I always lived below my means. The only debt I had was my mortgage, and by having a roommate, I kept my cost of living very manageable. Again, this was not by accident.

I was laid off a second time, and I went on vacation! I had been working in a very toxic work environment. A blunder devastated the company, and 30% of the company was let go. I remember distinctly getting into my car with my box of stuff and smiling, thinking that I would never have to go back into that building. My first phone call was to a friend so we could celebrate! I packed my bags, went on vacation, and took another few weeks off before looking for a job. Having savings is crucial to financial success and peace of mind, especially during emergencies. Had I needed money, I could have easily used credit cards to get by, essentially digging a financial hole. How many years would it take to pay off those credit cards?

Imagine the stress that would have caused. Maybe you don't need to imagine that. Perhaps you have been in that boat. Having savings did not keep life from throwing curveballs, but it did soften the blow.

As I write this, we are experiencing a world pandemic that has effectively shut down entire industries: tourism and restaurants, movies, sports, entertainment of all sorts, and countless others. Across the world, we are hunkering down in our homes, trying to keep this virus, COVID-19, from overwhelming our healthcare facilities. We are facing record-breaking unemployment rates. Knowing that so many Americans live paycheck to paycheck, this will be financially devastating. And none of us knows how long this will last or what the implications will be down the line. That makes this part of financial planning so crucial. When we save, we can't ever know how much savings is enough. We save to lessen the blow of whatever comes our way. Saving came naturally to me, but as I said before, I did not like spending the money I had saved. It pained me to part with it, even if it was for a good or necessary reason. And my husband saw money in the account as money worth spending. After quite a bit of trial and error, we came up with a way to alleviate my anxiety and stop overspending. We created a solid plan for how to spend our savings by using Savings Buckets. These buckets were just additional savings accounts in our bank. Most people open one checking account and one savings account, but we have several individual savings accounts to keep money separated physically. Although I often get questioned about my method, it has worked so well for us that I tell everyone about it, and it might just help you reach your own goals.

Just like you need to plan how to spend your money, you need to plan how to save it. Below are the savings accounts we have set up and seem to need the most, although, at times, we have added accounts as our needs changed. Read through and think about how setting up separate savings accounts for different goals can help you. I suggest starting with the first three. The rest you can decide with your partner, but ***do not jeopardize your future by skimping on your savings. Saving is the key to creating a secure financial future.*** These can change as your needs change. It is OK (and really good) to reevaluate and make changes to these accounts over time.

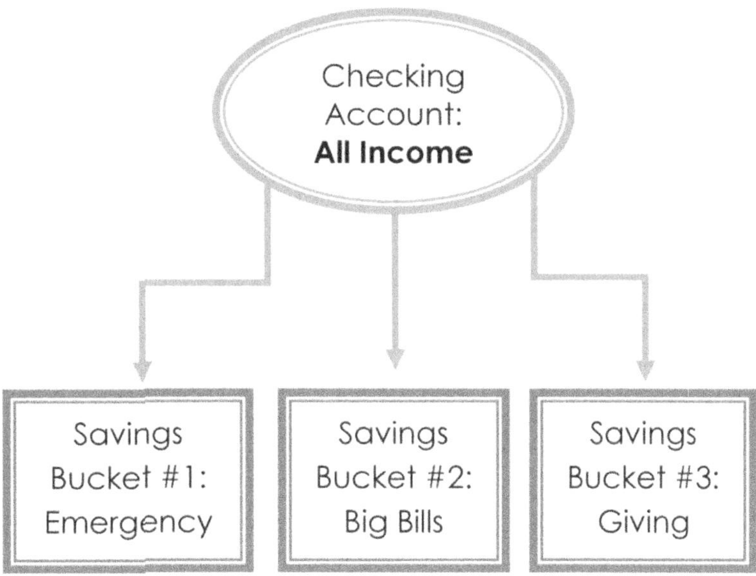

Bucket #1: *Emergency Savings — Minimum 3-6 months of expenses*

I mentioned how my emergency savings saved my bacon twice before I was married. **Fully fund this account before any other.** Then, once you hit your target amount, continue automatic transfers of a lesser amount, and keep building up this account. Then, do not use this money unless it is an actual emergency. Think about your specific job and field of work. Would you be able to find a job quickly, or would it take some time? The balance in this account has to do with your comfort level. Some people won't feel comfortable with less than eight to twelve months of expenses. Others think that they can jump right into another job, and three months' savings is OK. However, you might be able to cover a job loss with two or three months of savings, but if you were somehow *unable* to go back to work quickly, you'd be happy you kept saving. An illness or injury can prevent you from going back to work AND flood you with medical bills.

Emergency *noun, often attributive* emer·gen·cy | \ i-ˈmər-jən(t)-sē \

1: an unforeseen combination of circumstances or the resulting state that calls for immediate action

2: an urgent need for assistance or relief

An emergency is not a bill you forgot about, not an expense you didn't plan for, but an event you didn't know was coming. If you are still unsure if your expense is an emergency, please use this handy flow chart. Go ahead and make a copy of this flowchart and keep it handy.

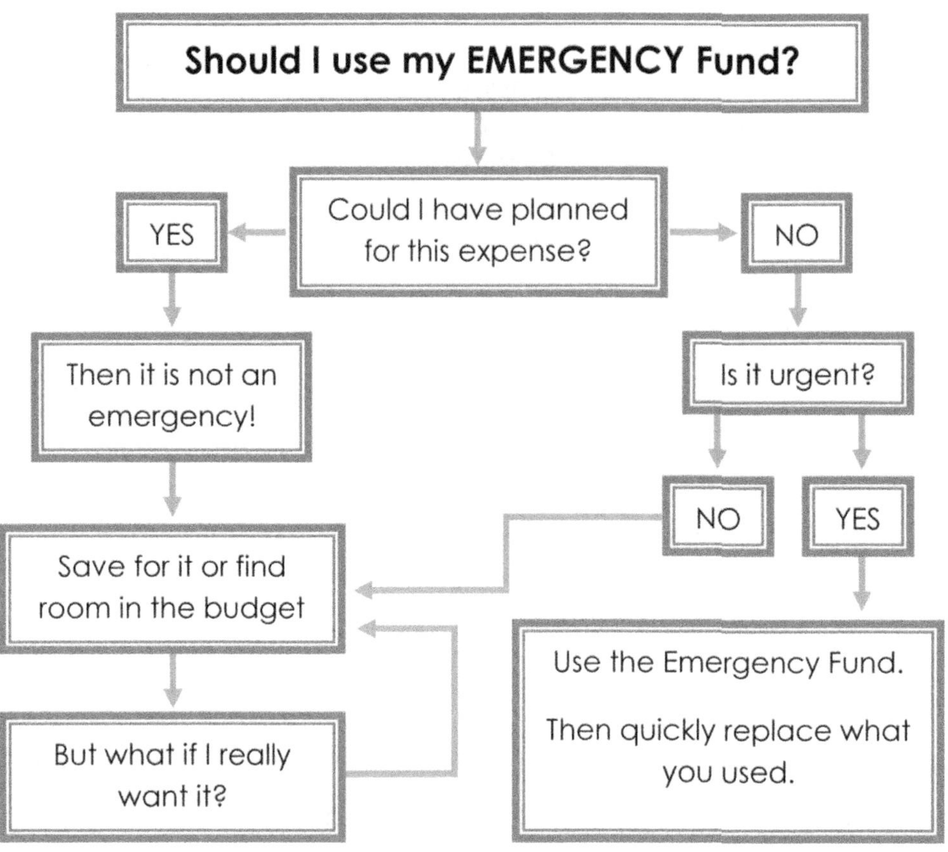

Looking at the Common Monthly Expenses Worksheet. Add up all of your monthly expenses, minus what you are putting into savings.

What is the total of your monthly expenses? $_________

How many months of expenses do you need to feel secure?_________months

Bucket #2: *Big Bills — Bills that are due 1 – 2 times a year*

This bucket or savings account is sometimes referred to as a "sinking fund." It will keep you from using your emergency fund for bills that are not an emergency. Think about the large bills you have due a few times a year, such as your home insurance, property taxes, car insurance, registration, repairs, (estimate the costs of oil changes and tires) and anything else that you pay in lump sums. Let's say your total of all those yearly bills is $3600. Divided by twelve months is $300/month. Set up an auto-transfer or transfers to get a total of $300 a month deposited into your account for large bills. You might be able to have the entire amount come out of your first or second paycheck. Maybe you want to split it between paychecks.

Whatever way you decide to fund your account is OK, ***as long as it is automatic.*** Do not be tempted to contribute less for any reason. When it comes due, transfer the bill amount to your checking account to pay it. It feels less like a payment because it was already set aside for that specific reason. It already had a job. In your mind, it was already gone!

For me, this was the ultimate relief. I wasn't jeopardizing my future for tires and car insurance! Suddenly, I would get a bill and not blink twice about it. The sick feeling I used to have as I paid it was gone! Thousands of dollars could leave this account, and it no longer stressed me out. These dollars were just doing their job!

Bucket #2a: *Medical*

If your medical expenses are significant, it is a good idea to save for medical bills separately to track payments efficiently. These expenses might qualify as a tax write-off, so keep track. However, if your medical expenses are low, and you are young and healthy, estimate what you use in a year and add it to your Big Bills fund. Like the other bills, calculate how much you'll need each year and set up an auto-transfer to your Medical Account from your checking account each month. If your company offers a Health Savings Account (HSA), please talk to your human resources about how to set this up. When you set up an HSA account, the monthly amount you have estimated your medical expenses to be will be taken out of your paycheck each month before you are taxed. Your taxable income will be less, meaning that you will pay fewer taxes! And using tax-deferred money is like getting a discount on medical expenses! Whether you set up a medical savings bucket or use an HSA account, only use it for medical expenses.

Go back to your Common Monthly Expenses Worksheet and highlight every bill due only a few times a year. Usually, property taxes, car registration, and insurance bills fall into this category, but you might have others, like gym memberships. Next, highlight what you have estimated your car repairs, medical bills, and other irregular expenses. Add all of this up.

What is the total yearly amount of all your big bills? $__________yearly

How much do you need to put on auto save each month? $__________yearly

Will you save in one lump sum, with each paycheck, or each week?

____

____

____

Bucket #3: *Giving — Gifts and Charity*

I like to make this its own bucket so that it is clear how much money I can spend on birthdays, charities, and the holidays! Whatever is in that account, this is your MAX gift budget. Giving isn't supposed to stress you out, and by no means should it put you in debt! ***Repeat after me, "I will not put gifts on a credit card."***

When I get a call or email about a fundraiser, I love that I just transfer the money from this savings account into my checking account to pay it. I never have to look at my budget and think, "OK, what can I give this kid to run laps at school?" or "Oh man, I feel so sorry for this family who needs help, butI just can't swing it." It doesn't affect my budget because the money in this account is for someone else. This money doesn't belong to me anymore. I am just a keeper until I know who needs it. It is my Fairy Godmother Fund. The Giving bucket is my favorite account.

How much do you need to save each month for gifts and charity? $__________monthly

You might be dismissing me and thinking of all the points you will rack up on that credit card. Remember, *no one gets rich from credit card points.* Think about what kinds of debts you have right now. If you are struggling to pay down credit cards, this is not a viable option for you. Think about how you can change the behavior and habits that may have gotten you into a less than ideal situation. Use money from your checking or savings bucket, and use your debit card to pay for all your purchases going forward.

The easiest way to stop emergencies from derailing your life is by funding separate bank accounts for expenses that you know and **don't know** are coming. Preparing will cut down on your financial stress in a **huge, huge** way. **Set up your bank with AUTO-TRANSFERS to separate savings accounts each month** to fund each of your goals, emergencies, and future. You can thank yourself later.

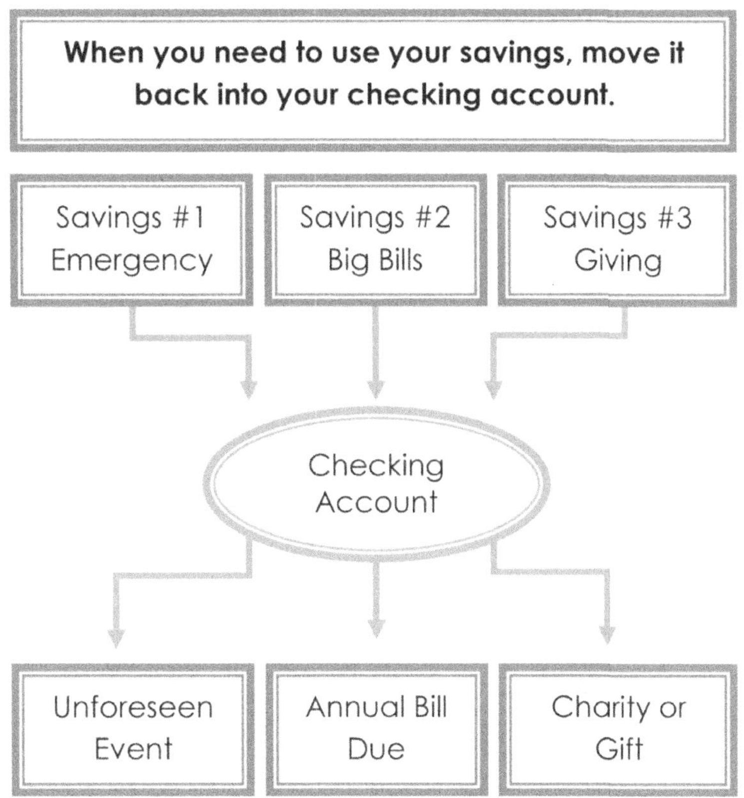

Start with the top three Savings Buckets—**Emergency, Big Bills, and Giving**—and see where it takes you. I will talk about spending buckets next. After the fiasco of our previous car-buying experience, I am determined to pay cash for any cars we buy in the future so one of my Savings Buckets is for future cars. However, since this is a long-term savings that I will not need for several years, I have put the money into a safe investment fund to make some money off of my savings! I have yet another account for home renovation projects. While cooking is not for me, I love a good renovation, so I like to save up for the big projects. I also have rental property, so I have separate emergency savings for that. Think about what you need to live your life and customize this list for your own needs. Once you have a handle on all of this, one account can hold several categories. For example, my Big Bills account might also hold savings for home projects and a new computer. Let's say you have decided that in addition to the money you are saving for big bills, you have budgeted to save $50 extra for a home project and $50 extra for a computer. Track the breakdown by making a note on your budget sheet each month with each category's total. Sometimes it's just easier to have separate accounts, especially if you or your partner tends to spend what is available or are not diligent about notes. Know yourself and adjust accordingly.

Only after you have your emergency savings funded, and your big bills accounts are on autopilot, will you start putting aside money for retirement. Your emergency savings and big bills account determine your quality of life now, while your retirement savings will determine your quality of life in retirement. You do not want to drag your feet on this. Figuring out how to balance living your best life now, and saving enough to retire can be tricky, but we will go through it step-by-step. I will talk to you a little more about retirements later.

PLANNING FOR SPENDING

Being a finance hero doesn't start with numbers. It begins with emotions. Now that you have some more insights into what you learned and believe about money, you will look at how spending money makes you feel. There is a method the Japanese use called kakeibo. Japanese culture is well known for being mindful, respectful, and thoughtful. It is no wonder that the Japanese culture, as a whole, is incredibly financially stable. This method, kakeibo, was created by a woman named Hani Motoko and has been in practice in Japan for over 100 years. Her idea was to take a simple journal and with bullet points, write down all purchases made. Have you ever had money in your wallet, and then after a few stops, it is all gone, and you have nothing to show for it? Maybe you got gas and stopped in for a Slurpee, then that afternoon, got a coffee and pastry for an afternoon pick-me-up, then on and on. Scientists have proven that by handwriting something, it gets into your brain. These are the things you want in your brain.

Think back on the last day or two, and write down everything you bought. Did you pay with cash or put it on a credit card? Next to it, rate it with the feeling you had then, and the feeling you have now. Wereyou happy, anxious, stressed, or indifferent? Did that feeling last? Are they the same today? Did you buy something that satisfied some instant gratification, and now you are indifferent toward it or regretting it?

As you go on, think about this before you even buy something. Think about how long that feeling will last. Is this something that you need? Will you use it, or will it end up collecting dust or being donated? Is it something you can live without? Did you go shopping for it, or did you just come across it? Do you have space for it? The Kakeibo Method is an excellent practice for understanding why you spend. Many "needs" are actually "wants," and once you know the difference, you'll be able to stick to your budget better.

Make a list of all your purchases in the last two days:

Purchase	*Cash or Credit*	*Feeling at Time of Purchase*	*Feeling Two Days Later*

TRAVEL AND PER DIEM SPENDING

Spending money is necessary, and if you plan, you can pay for some fantastic opportunities. When I ask people what they would do if money were no issue, the number one answer I get is travel! Automatically transfer money into your travel bucket each month. Whether you have determined a destination or not, start putting money into this account automatically every month, even if you can only begin with $10 or $20 a month. As you decide when and where you are going, make sure you have all the money in your travel account to pay for it. All of it. Using your emergency fund for a vacation asks for huge trouble, and paying for it on a credit card is stressful AND more expensive. ***Repeat after me: "I will not put my vacation on a credit card."***

How much will I put away each month for travel? $__________monthly

Travel is a significant and often budget-killing expense, and yet, it can be so fulfilling if it isn't stressing you out. When planning a trip, you need to understand how much you expect it to cost you. This requires research. How much will it cost you to get there? Do you need to fly, or can you drive? How much will you need to pay for gas? Will you need to pay for airport parking? When you get there, can you buy groceries and make your meals, or will you be eating out? What activities will you be participating in? Are you going on tours? Will you need extra gear for hiking or camping? Are you traveling out of the country? What is the exchange rate?

Once you have researched and budgeted to the best of your ability, make sure that you have saved enough for your trip. Paying for big items like plane tickets and lodging ahead of time is a good idea. After your predetermined expenses are taken care of, decide how much cash you want to spend on food and other activities while you are on your trip and divide it out as per diem. For example, you are going to Rome for five days. Your flight lands at 9 a.m. on your first day, and you have set aside $500 spending money. This is easy! You will have $100 per day to spend on whatever you want! You sit down and enjoy your first meal at a cafe overlooking ancient ruins, with the sun out and the wine flowing...and your firstmeal just cost you $85. *Ouch.* It is a panini stand for lunch and dinner! You are going to have to rethink that tour you wanted to take that afternoon. You can absolutely spend more than $100 on any given dayto do something worthwhile, making sure that overall, you are sticking to your maximum $500 spendingcash allowance.

Per diem doesn't have to apply to just travel either. Let's say you have budgeted $750 for gas and groceries each month, giving you a per diem of $25 a day. On the first day of the month, you might get gas AND groceries, totaling $100. You just spent four days worth of money! Don't panic. The likelihood of you needing to buy either gas or groceries in the next few days is low. And if you find yourself in a situation where you are getting to the bottom of your cupboard or gas tank, get creative and cook something from the freezer or make a pasta extravaganza. Combine errands, so you aren't using gas unnecessarily.

What per diems can you put in place to help you stay on budget?

____

____

____

____

____

Over time, you'll learn the natural rhythm of your life. You will have a more intuitive feeling about what you can spend. These exercises help fine tune that.

INSURANCE

Oh, the insurance you need! The sole purpose of having insurance is to offset the financial burden. For example, we have car insurance just in case we cause damage to someone else's car. These costs can add up very quickly. If we have adequate coverage, our out-of-pocket costs will be significantly less than if we had to pay for all the damages.

Liability *noun* li·a·bil·i·ty | līə'bilədē/

1. the state of being responsible for something, especially by law.

"The partners accept unlimited **liability for** any risks they undertake."

Similar: accountability, responsibility, legal responsibility, answerability, incrimination, blame, blameworthiness, culpability

In other words, ***liability is debt waiting to happen!*** When we look at our lives, we have many areas where we have some risk of paying for a considerable expense. The most common ones people have are health, home, and auto. However, you could be leaving yourself wide open to a big problem if you don't cover all of the areas in life where you have exposure. Make sure you have adequate coverage in each of these areas: Life, Health, Home, Auto, Disability, Identity, Long-Term, and Umbrella Insurance. For a relatively small amount, you are offsetting your risk should something significant happen. One car accident or hospital stay can devastate your finances. Selling your home, moving in with family, or worse, isn't what you need to be dealing with during an already difficult time. As we go along, we will evaluate your insurance needs . ***Inadequate insurance can bankrupt you.***

What would happen if your bills from injury or illness were more than your emergency fund?

____

____

____

____

____

What if you could never work again?

What would happen to your family if you died?

Where do you think you need coverage in your life?

As you are shopping for any kind of insurance, look at the entire package. Low premiums can mean high deductibles, or it might limit your network. For instance, your monthly bill, or your premium, is small, but a car accident out-of-pocket deductible could be very high, similarly with doctors. Compare price, coverage, network, and out-of-pocket expenses. Call multiple companies or one that compares several for you. Make sure that you are comparing pricing for the same amount of coverage. These can be confusing when you start out. The best advice I can give is to tell the first person you talk to that you aren't sure what you need or can afford and ask them to walk you through it. If it is still confusing, guess what, you can tell the next person you talk to the same thing. Not all insurance agents have a knack for explaining their options well, so if this is new territory for you, don't blindly sign up for something you don't understand. Keep asking. Take notes. And then, in a year or so, do it again. Pricing guidelines can change so that you could find a better rate for the same coverage. Also, talk to companies that can insure multiple policies. Insuring your car and home with the same company could earn you a discounted rate.

Life Insurance

If you have anyone depending on your income to live on or are a stay-at-home or single parent, you needed life insurance yesterday. This is non-negotiable. Do not put off until you have more money. Life insurance is so important! Leaving your loved ones without a financial safety net is the worst thing that can happen if you were to die. And yes, even if you don't bring in an income, you still need life insurance. Why? If you take care of your young children while your spouse goes to work every day and then you die, your spouse will need to hire someone to watch the kids, take them to school, and maybe even clean your house! Some of the stories I have heard about this haunt me. You do not want your family to be someone's cautionary tale. Protect them.

Generally speaking, you need twelve to twenty times your annual income for a term life insurance policy. The good news is that these are not very expensive, and the younger you are when you get one, the less it is. Get one with a **fixed rate.** Think about your kids' ages and your liabilities, such as a mortgage or other debt. Typically, when kids are young, you need a twenty-year term policy so that by the time they no longer need to rely on you to take care of them, your policy is coming to an end. The older your kids are, the less debt you have, the less insurance you need. Remember, the more financially independent you are, you become what is called "self-insured." Meaning you can cover all that stuff with your savings. Until that day, get the best insurance you can afford! Insure yourself for what you can't pay for out of pocket if something does happen.

Questions to ask before getting life insurance:

1. *What is the monthly/annual cost?*
2. *Is there a waiting period before the plan goes into effect?*
3. *Are there circumstances in which benefits are not paid?*
4. *What happens if a payment is late or missed?*
5. *Can the insurance company cancel your policy?*
6. *How and when are benefits paid out?*
7. *Whom do I contact with questions after the policy is in effect?*

Health Insurance

Are you breathing? Then you need health insurance. And yes, this can be quite costly. If your job doesn't offer health insurance, at least look into catastrophic coverage which can be considerably less per month than health insurance. It only covered major traumas, but we all know how costly a hospital stay can be. Shop around and find room in your budget to get full coverage health insurance.

When you are shopping for insurance, make sure that if you have doctors that you want to keep, that they will be available and at what cost. If you have money saved in an emergency fund, you could opt for a lower premium and higher deductibles. That goes for most insurances. Once you have a robust safety net, you can afford to pay more when something goes wrong, and save money on your monthly premium.

Questions to ask about your medical insurance:

1. *What will I have to pay out of pocket? Yearly? Lifetime?*
2. *Can you pick your own doctors, or do you need to choose from their list?*
3. *Are other benefits included, like dental, vision, or prescriptions?*
4. *Are there any restrictions, like going to the ER if I am out of town?*
5. *Are routine medical exams, like yearly exams, covered?*
6. *Are there restrictions on pre-existing conditions?*

Home/Renters Insurance

Your home and personal property are huge assets, and you need to protect them. If you rent, your landlord isn't responsible for your items should something happen, like a fire or flood. In fact, your landlord may not be allowed to cover your belongings. The good news is that Renters Insurance is pretty inexpensive and is a lot cheaper than replacing all of your belongings.

First, you'll need to estimate the cost of your belongings. Insurance companies can help you with a rough estimate. If you have something of great value, like a collection, antiques, or jewelry, get an appraisal done and specifically cover it in your insurance policy. Take pictures or videos of your belongings and upload them online to access it if you need to show proof for insurance. Be sure you update it every year.

Here are some questions to ask when searching for homeowners insurance:

1. *If my home is destroyed, what would it cost to cover rebuilding it?*
2. *Will it cover hotel costs if I am displaced from my home?*
3. *How much are my belongings (furniture/appliances/clothing) worth?*
4. *How much liability insurance do I need?*
5. *Are there discounts for burglar alarms or cameras?*
6. *How much is the deductible on a claim?*

Here are some questions to ask when searching for renter's insurance:

1. *What personal property is covered?*
2. *Will it cover damage from storms?*
3. *What happens if someone gets hurt in my house?*
4. *Does my insurance cover roommates or dogs?*
5. *Are my belongings, like laptops or bikes, covered if they are stolen outside of my house?*
6. *How much is the deductible on a claim?*

Car Insurance

If you drive, then you need car insurance. Like the others, shop around. Know what you can afford as far as a deductible. Car insurance is the most expensive for new drivers or drivers with accidents and tickets. There isn't anything you can do about your age, but as you get some years of driving experience and have a good driving record, you could be eligible for a decrease in your premium. What surprised me was that your credit score could also affect your costs! So, if you are looking at a lower-than-ideal credit score right now, call and see what your car insurance could drop once you have improved your credit score. Other possible discounts include paying in full once a year, having anti-theft or other safety features built into your car. Ask about how you can qualify.

Do not let your coverage lapse! Being uninsured for any period will hurt the rate you pay for car insurance. Keep your auto-insurance on auto-pay. If you pay it once or twice a year, make sure you auto-transfer the money you need to pay it on time from your Big Bill savings account. Oh, and that fancy sports car you want to buy? The chances are that the insurance will be on the higher side, so consider that before making a purchase.

Questions to ask when buying car insurance:

1. *How much liability insurance do I need?*
2. *Are there discounts that I can qualify for or work toward?*
3. *What is covered if I am in an accident or my car is damaged?*
4. *What is covered if someone is injured or dies?*
5. *How much personal injury protection do I have?*
6. *What medical payments are covered?*
7. *How much uninsured/underinsured motorist coverage do I need?*
8. *Does it cover disability? Work or income loss?*
9. *Are there accidental death benefits? Funeral expenses?*
10. *What are my out-of-pocket expenses?*

Identity Insurance

Identity theft is skyrocketing, and it can cost you a lot of time and money. Identity insurance can cost less than $10 a month if you pay for the whole year upfront. Make sure that it isn't just a credit monitoring system. These are pretty useless. I was using one that did not alert me to the judgment on the accountI found when I was buying my first house. When I canceled, they had the nerve to tell me that I would regret it because something could get on my credit report without my knowing about it.

After some internet searching and review reading, I found one that will RECOVER identity as well as monitor. Recovering your identity can take many hundreds of hours and be quite costly. For such a low amount each month, it is well worth getting identity insurance.

Make sure that it monitors all three credit bureaus: TransUnion, Experian, and Equifax. As with all insurance, call several and compare. Find out exactly what they cover and don't cover. Find out if you'll have to pay for anything out of pocket. See if you can add family members, and at what cost. You are going to be a pro at this. Be open to learning and ask as many questions as you need to feel comfortable.

Questions to ask when shopping for identity insurance:

1. *What does this identity insurance cover?*
2. *Does it recover identities or just monitor?*
3. *Does it monitor all three credit bureaus?*
4. *What does it cost per month? Per year?*

Disability Insurance

Disability insurance is one of the most important and most neglected of all insurance coverage. Because I cannot stress enough how vital disability insurance is, I will show you some facts straight from DisabilityCanHappen.org (2018):

https://disabilitycanhappen.org/disability-statistic/

Disability statistics

- *Only 48% of American adults have enough savings to cover three months of living expenses in the event they're not earning any income.*
- *More than 25% of people can expect to be out of work for at least a year because of a disabling condition before they reach normal retirement age.*
- *Primary reasons for filing bankruptcy: medical bills (26%), lost job (20%), illness or injury on part of self or family members (15%).*
- *Cancer patients were 2.65 times more likely to go bankrupt than people without cancer, with younger (under age fifty) cancer patients having the highest rates of bankruptcy.*
- *Workers' Compensation only covers time away from work if the disabling illness or injury was directly work-related. In 2016, only 1% of American workers missed work because of an occupational illness or injury.*
- *From 2006 to 2015, only 34% of Social Security Disability Insurance (SSDI) claimants had their applications approved. Of those, 11% had to file for appeal.*

- *It generally takes three to five months from the time of application for benefits to get an initial decision. Case appeal processing time averages more than eighteen months.*

- *The average disability benefit as of January 2018 was $1,197 a month. That equates to $14,364 annually—barely above the poverty guideline of $12,140 for a one-person household, and below the guideline of $16,640 for a two-person household.*

- The most common reasons for **short-term** disability claims are ***pregnancies, physical injuries and fractures, digestive disorders, such as hernias and gastritis, and mental health issues including depression and anxiety***.

- The most common reasons for **long-term** disability claims are ***pregnancies, physical injuries and fractures, cancer, and mental health issues including depression and anxiety***. None of these are unusual ailments and Workers' Compensation and Social Security do not cover most of these challenges.

If you are a full-time employee, you may already have short-term disability provided by the state you live in. With all that said, get additional or supplemental disability insurance! Shop around. Buy the most you can afford. Short-term disability insurance will typically cover 60 to 80% of your income, so you'll still need that emergency fund. Especially since some policies will take some time to start paying you after the incident claim, find out if your policy has a waiting period. Make sure you purchase non-cancelable, renewable, and "Occupational" or "Own OCC" coverage, which covers the job you were trained to do. For example, you are a transcriber and you lose mobility in your hands and can no longer type. You may be able to get another job doing something else, but disability insurance will help you if you can't do your job. And another job may not pay you as well, have hours you want, or the benefits you need.

Questions to ask about disability insurance:

1. *Do I already have short term disability included in my employment?*
2. *Do I need short or long-term insurance? Should I get both?*
3. *Is this Occupational Insurance?*
4. *What will this insurance cover? What will it not cover?*
5. *How much of my income will it cover?*
6. *When will I start receiving benefits?*

7. *How long will I receive benefits?*

Long Term Care Insurance

Once you are sixty, invest in long-term care insurance. Nearly 70% of us will need to be in a nursing home for an extended time. These facilities are costly and can cost over $100,000 per year! Cover yourself so your family isn't left trying to figure out how to pay for your care. Long-term care insurance isn't cheap. Policies can be several hundred dollars per month. Again, they can vary depending on your age, policy coverage, and other factors. Also, policy prices will begin to increase once you are over sixty. If this is you, start shopping around, and if you are younger, keep this in mind for when that day rolls around. It is better to pay a few hundred dollars a month versus the several thousand dollars a month that care facilities can cost.

Unfortunately, there isn't an easy way to spell out how much long-term coverage you'll need. Your comfort level will be a big part of how you determine what coverage you should have. There are several considerations to keep in mind. Take a look at your family history and how long your family members tend to live. Do debilitating diseases run in your family? Or do you have any ailments that will require specialized help in your later years? How much do you have saved for your retirement? Think about if you will need to move to be closer to family. Call a few retirement homes and interview them. Find out what services they offer and how much it costs to live there. Is the price of care fixed, or will it go up each year? Knowing these costs will help give you an idea of monthly expenses. When you talk to an agent, ask them how they determine how much coverage is needed. And remember, talk to several different companies. The more questions you ask, the more people you talk to, the better decision you'll make.

What genetic components should you take into consideration when thinking about your golden years?

Questions to ask when shopping for Long Term Care Insurance?

1. *What is the best way to calculate how much coverage I will need?*
2. *How long should I insure myself?*
3. *When will coverage start?*
4. *Does my health history affect coverage?*

Umbrella Policy

Once you begin building wealth and have more significant assets, you'll want to protect yourself with an umbrella policy. Again, talk to your agent to determine how much coverage you will need. Umbrella policies cover you above and beyond your other insurance, but it does not take the place of any of the other policies. You will need to show proof of coverage to qualify for an umbrella policy. It works like this: let's say you are in a car accident and someone sues you for 1.2 million dollars, but your car insurance only covers 1 million. Your umbrella policy will cover the other $200,000. How would you pay $200,000 if you were to be sued? So, you can see how important this is, even if you have all your other insurance policies in place. Once you start acquiring wealth, this is a must.

Questions to ask when shopping for an umbrella policy:

1. *Will claims be "paid on behalf," meaning that the insurance company will pay expenses directly, or will I be reimbursed after paying for expenses out of pocket?*
2. *How much will I have to pay out of pocket per claim?*
3. *What exactly is covered in this policy?*
4. *What isn't covered in this policy?*

Pet Insurance

If you have pets, please consider getting them insured. We all love our pets, and a single trip to the vet can be several hundred dollars. If you do not have a fully funded emergency fund of a minimum of three to six months' worth of monthly expenses, please get pet insurance. Once you have your emergency fund in place, you can decide with your accountability partner whether or not you would rather pay for vet bills out of pocket or continue to pay for insurance. Talk to your vet about this and get their advice for coverage on your pet.

This is your life to protect, so use this list to get the insurance you need. Direct your questions to insurance agents, do internet searches. Talk to multiple agents before picking a plan. Review your coverage from time to time. It isn't on the top of my to-do list either, but it is crucial and should be done about once a year, just like your doctor check-ups. Mark it on your calendar for a month that isn't typically crazy for you. If you know that March is full of birthdays and your anniversary, then maybe April is a better time for your annual Insurance Check-In. Make it a recurring event on your calendar and stick to it. The peace of mind that comes when you know your insurance will cover whatever life can throw at you and is worth every penny.

Thirteen percent of personal liability awards and settlements hit the million-dollar mark or higher. — Jury Verdict Research

RETIREMENT

One of the biggest anxieties people talk to me about revolves around their retirement. Most people I talk to are not confident they will have enough to retire comfortably. I was one of these people. My husband was not so concerned. He had a rough running tab of his retirement accounts that he had from jobs before we had met in his head. He wasn't worried about it in the least. Once I had a statement from each fund in our files, I could breathe a lot easier. It also gave us the information to monitor our assets.

I still didn't know ***how to evaluate*** how we were doing. I asked our financial advisor, and he gave me an answer so vague that it was no help whatsoever. Then I started doing some of my own research. I found lots of calculators. I would put in what we had, what we were contributing monthly, and how many more years we had before retirement. It would spit out a number with zero explanation. Was it enough? I had no idea.

Finally, I came across a "Rule of Thumb" page that told me we would need about twenty times our annual income to retire. WHOA! What a very scary moment in my financial life! How in the world could someone possibly save that much money? Once I was over my initial shock, it made sense. Let's say you retire at sixty-seven. If you have twenty years of income, you should be OK if you die around eighty-seven. Sounds good? But what if you live longer or retire sooner? Or what if you still have a home mortgage to pay for or had significant medical expenses? Well, at least I had a starting point. Knowing that all my grandparents lived pretty long lives, I decided to shoot for twenty-five years of retirement, so I had to make sure I had twenty-five times my annual income. Except, I still had to figure out how to save that much money.

In an ideal world, you would begin investing 15-20% of your income from your very first paycheck into a 401(k), Roth IRA, or a mutual fund. So, if you are sixteen years old, being supported by your parents, and mowing lawns over the summer, you could invest all or most of your income into a retirement account. Why in the world would a person start saving for retirement at age sixteen? Well, because of the miracle of compound interest. When you invest your money into an account with compound interest, you earn interest on the money you put into your account, and then you earn interest on the interest. Why not just put that money in a savings account? I am glad you asked. **The average savings account will earn .06% interest.** Our nation's largest banks pay you even less. It is crucial that you earn compound interest on your retirement savings of at least 7%.

For example, if you invest $100 at 10% **simple interest**, you would earn 10%, or $10 each year, on your investment. At the end of eight years, you'll have your original $100 plus $80 in interest, totaling $180.

If you put that same $100 into an account earning the same 10%, but this time it is **compound interest**, something very different happens. In the first year, you'll make the same $10, but in the second year, you'll receive 10% on $110. Each year, you'll make more money because your balance is higher. At the end of the same eight years, you'll have a total of $214.50. Would you rather have $180 or $214.50? And that is after eight years, with only $100. Imagine what would happen if you put in $100 each month into that account, over forty years. That is what you'll be doing when investing in your retirement savings into accounts with compound interest.

If that is still a little confusing or you don't think it is that big of a deal, check out these two women's stories.

Anna's parents taught her at a young age how important it is to save for retirement. She begins putting away $400 every month ($4,800 a year) from the time she turns eighteen until she turns sixty-seven.

Zoe's parents assume she will start saving for retirement once she has graduated from college and has a full-time job, but never actually have a conversation with her about it. Zoe doesn't put any thought into retirement until she is thirty years old. She starts putting away $1,042 every month ($12,500 a year, $7,700 more per year than what Anna contributes each year) until she turns sixty-seven.

Anna invests a total of $240,000 of her own money.

Zoe invests a total of $475,000 of her own money.

Both women end up with **three million dollars** in their retirement funds, but Zoe had to invest almost double what Anna did. Anna used years to her advantage.

Albert Einstein famously said, ***"Compound interest is the eighth wonder of the world. He who understands it, earns it; he who doesn't, pays it."*** Benjamin Franklin explains this very simply, saying, ***"Money makes money. And the money that money makes, makes money."*** And who doesn't want to make money just by having money? Credit card companies have mastered making money that makes money. Do you want to pay it or earn it?

If you are just starting out, start investing immediately.

If you are fifty years old and haven't started investing, start now. If you have young people in your life, encourage them to begin investing now. Tell them the story of these two women; help them understand what they gain when they start early, and lose by procrastination. And by the way, neither of these women maxed out their 401(k). Currently, each person can put $19,500 each year into a 401(k). People over fifty years old are allowed to contribute an extra $6,500 per year. This number can change from year to year, so find out what the current year's contribution max is for you.

From reading this book, you know that we did not consistently invest 15-20% of our income. But sticking our heads in the sand and hoping for the best was not going to cut it. First, we had to figure out what we needed for retirement. I took our annual salary and multiplied it by twenty-five. I started by putting my eyeballs back in my head. Then, I found a decent online calculator. I like this one: https://www.nerdwallet.com/investing/retirement-calculator.

Play with the numbers, and you will see very quickly what you'll need to work towards, and if you are meeting that goal or not. If you are not, you can plug in some numbers and find out what you need to contribute each month to achieve that goal. Go ahead and put in .06% and see what your savings account will earn for you. It will be a pretty grim number even compared to the 6% NerdWallet uses as a default. This is a low estimate by most standards but it is far better to be conservative and have more money saved than to plug in 15% or 20%. These will show you impressive numbers but are not realistic, and the last thing you want is to short-change yourself. The stock market has had a historical average of 10%. Of course, your money must stay in the stock market for many years to ensure that average. The last twenty years had an 8% return but had large swings of highs and lows. Use your judgment and as the years go on, make sure you are on track and make adjustments as needed.

Use an online calculator or app to plug in your numbers:

*What rate of return are you using?*_______%

*How much does it predict you should have at age sixty-seven? $*___________________

Is it at least twenty times your current annual salary?What

adjustments do you need to make?

Will you need to find another source for retirement income?

How do you feel about this exercise? Are you starting to sweat right now thinking you are never going to be able to save enough? It turns out that we would have been short upon retirement at the rate we were going, and I would not have known until it was too late. If you are short of making your goal like we were, go back to brainstorming on cutting back on expenses or making more money. Again, your goal is to do both. We quickly made changes to our budget to increase contributions to our 401(k) and found other ways to make active and passive income. **Active income** is what you get paid for a job. It takes your time and energy. **Passive income** pays you when you are sick, on vacation, or retired, whether you are working or not. It can take quite a bit of work to get going, but once the ball is rolling, it should be a minimal effort on your part. A few examples of passive income can be rental income, putting an advertisement on your car, selling courses or digital documents online, or creating an app. There are no limits to what you can set up for yourself. When you have a decent stream of passive income, several things happen:

First, financial emergencies become merely inconveniences.

Second, your stress levels decrease dramatically.

Third, you can speed up your retirement savings, taking advantage of compound interest. And

Fourth, you will need less money to retire because you will still be getting paid.

The number one tip I can give you for retirement is to ***find ways to replace the income from your job.*** And if you started saving for retirement later in life, this is your ticket out of despair. Work on your side hustle until it makes money for you while you sleep.

If you are thinking right now that there is no way you can make enough money to make your retirement a reality, pause, take a deep breath, and remember, your brain believes you! So, turn your thoughts around this very instant. This is your life! The only one truly stopping you is you. According to US News, 88% of millionaires are self-made, which means only 12% were born wealthy. Over 90% of self-made millionaires did so with real estate. Chances are, they started in average homes and had a thought, a dream, or a desire for a different life. They didn't tell themselves they couldn't do it, or it was too hard. They did one thing and then another, over and over, until they made it! And so can you! But you cannot do it by doing the same thing you have always done. Make changes to your fundamental beliefs, to your daily habits, and your actions. ***"An idiot with a plan can beat a genius without a plan." —Warren BuffetT***

Be the idiot with a plan!

Don't let any excuse stop you from investing in your future. The sooner you start, the more significant your benefit will be. There are plenty of ways to invest. Educate yourself. Here is some basic information about different options.

401(k): Offered at lots of companies for their employees, and sometimes will match up to a certain percentage. If your company matches, make sure you are at least investing that amount, so you aren't leaving free money on the table. These 401(k)s are funded with pre-tax money and taxed when you withdraw at whatever income bracket you fall into in the future. There are age restrictions and penalties for pulling out money before retirement age.

Roth IRA: Currently, if you make less than $124,000 a year as a single person or $196,000 for a married couple, you can open a Roth IRA and contribute up to $6,000 per year or $7,000 for people over fifty years old. This money goes in after you have paid income taxes, grows, and comes out tax-free.

SEP IRA: If you are self-employed, this is your opportunity to fund your future. You can contribute 25% of your income, up to $57,000 each year! Make sure you talk to a tax accountant to make sure you meet the qualifications for this type of IRA.

HSA: This Health Savings Plan is a real winner but should not be confused with an FSA, in which you need to "use it or lose it" each calendar year. If your employer offers an HSA, jump on it! You can contribute to it pre-taxed out of your paycheck. As long as you use this money for medical expenses, you never pay taxes on it. Whoa! You won't have to use your taxable 401(k) for medical costs!

Investment Brokerage Accounts: In this day and age, there is no reason for you not to open an investment account for the stock market. Fidelity, Charles Schwab, and E-Trade consistently rank highly, and anyone can open an account. With a call or online form, you can decide your general comfort level and invest your money into an individual or a group of stocks. Some stocks will go up, some will go down, but overall, the stock market is a great place to invest, and risk can be offset with mutual funds instead of individual stocks.

What retirement accounts do you have?

____

____

____

What retirement accounts does your job offer?

____

____

____

____

____

What accounts would you like to open?

____

____

____

____

____

This shortlist is to get you familiar with some common ways to invest. These numbers can change every year, so please, be diligent and do some research. There are entire books and websites dedicated to teaching people how and where to invest. If this is all new to you, keep learning. Start by talking to your Human Resource contact at work and finding out what you can contribute. Call one or several brokerage companies and ask someone to walk you through opening an investment account online. People are accommodating when you are giving them your money to hold. Don't be afraid to ask for help in understanding your options.

Pro tip: Once your money goes into an account for retirement, do not use it until you retire. Robbing yourself for today's wants or needs will cause you bigger struggles and hardship down the road.

COLLEGE

Repeat after me: ***"It is more important to save for my retirement than to pay for my kids' college."*** I know you want to do what is best for your kids and what is best isn't burdening them when you are old, sick, and needy. Some couples think that their kids will share caretaking duties, but the reality is that it will probably land on one or two of your kids to bear the brunt of your care. Having witnessed the extreme sacrifices that my parents, aunts, and uncles made when my grandparents were in their last years makes this topic much more important. The last years of your life don't need to add financial stress as well as emotional anxiety to your family. **You must have all of your own ducks in a row before saving for college**.

So, you are all set up for retirement, but you still haven't saved enough for college. Before you jump to getting loans, think about this first. Many financial advisors say you are to never, ever, under any circumstances, co-sign a loan, even for your child. Remember, unless you have taught your children how to handle money, they will probably flounder. Do you want them to start learning on a loan for many thousands of dollars? Do you want them to learn with your name and credit on the line?

Here is a list of current **average tuition** for different types of colleges per year (2020). Think about you or your child borrowing this amount of money each year for education. What makes the most sense for you when you look at your finances?

Private college	$37,000 per year
Public, out of state	$27,000 per year
Public, in state	$11,000 per year
Community college	$5,000 per year

If needed, encourage your kids to get the required classes out of the way at the local community or state college. Also, tech schools, apprenticeships, and other less conventional schooling are becoming more socially acceptable and are more affordable. But still, your kid gets excellent grades, and you want them to go to the best school. Fantastic! But be wise about it. They can transfer after two years to some super awesome school, and pay for two years of tuition, not four. When you interview for a job, they don't ask where you started school; they ask where you graduated. And if you have been paying attention to the news, you will have heard about the insane amount of student debt that is crippling people all over the country. Don't be a statistic. Get creative.

Using the average tuition prices above or a specific college tuition, how much will you need to save for your children's college fund?

____

____

____

If you are still cringing at the thought of your super smart kid going to a tech or community college, let's be clear: **A degree does not ensure success; only you can do that.**

You may have started with student loans yourself, or know people who felt the crushing weight of it as they got married and started families. If you fall into this category, what would you have done differently or the same? What advice do you wish you had gotten? There is not one answer to this, but some forethought and planning can do a lot to keep you or your kids from a hole that seems to have swallowed up the hopes of many Americans.

Let's say your child gets a scholarship, or you saved a lot of money for their education, making tuition manageable. Consider having them work part-time to pay living expenses in real-time. Lots of loans include the cost of living expenses. Please don't set yourself up to be paying for rent and groceries ten years from now because it was wrapped into a loan. Studies have shown that students who work part-time have better time management skills and get better grades. A person dedicated to their education will work to pay for it. Have you ever heard the expression, "having skin in the game?" It will be more valuable when they work hard to earn it. Sure, we want to help our kids, but sometimes helping them is letting them do it on their own.

Talk to your partner about your kids' college plan strategy and write it down.

Are you in agreement?

____

____

____

WILLS AND TRUSTS

If you aren't sure what the difference between a Will and a Trust is, you aren't alone. If you have a Will, it will take effect once you die, and your assets will pass through probate. Probate means that a court will look at your Will and make sure everything is valid and clear. Your assets will then be distributed to your heirs after a probate lawyer is paid well for doing their job. Having a Will states your wishes, but does not ensure that those wishes will come true if there is a legal reason standing in the way. Having a Will doesn't avoid probate.

Alternatively, a Trust takes effect when you set it up, so nothing happens to your money, property, and any other assets when you pass on. On paper, your Trust owns your assets, and you are the manager of that Trust. When you set it up, you'll assign a person or people to take over for you when you die or cannot manage it yourself. They become the new managers. None of your assets are redistributed or changes ownership. The new managers follow the wishes that you specify in the case of your death, usually through a Will that is included in the Trust. The new managers have the power to sell items or property or assign new managers. But the most significant difference is that your assets do not need to go through probate, so there are no fees involved when you die. Of course, you need to follow the correct steps and ensure that your assets are in the name of the Trust. For example, you already own a home, and then you set up a Trust. You must transfer the name on the title or deed of your home from your name to the name on the Trust. Amending the title is easy to do and is a common practice. Simply call your county recorder's office. Tell them you need to change the title of your home from your name into your Trust's name using a quitclaim deed form. They can help walk you through the process.

When you sit down to create your Will and Trust, you and your partner will need to make tough decisions. Some will be rather unpleasant to think about, like, if you were both to die, who will take care of your children? Who would have the power of attorney or medical directive if you are incapable of taking care of yourself? You will need to answer so many questions so ask the attorney for a list that you can go through ahead of time.

If you aren't sure exactly what you need to set up, talk to an Estate Lawyer. I know there are all kinds of DIY online options to create your own Wills and Trusts, but this is one area you want to make sure is 100% correct, so please, get a lawyer to draw up your Trust. If you should get it wrong, legally, your heirs could have a big problem. Lawyers are insured should they make a mistake. If a mistake costs you any money, your lawyer is liable to pay or correct it. But if you make a mistake, well, good luck if you die before you catch it. Your heirs might have a big problem on their hands.

Call an Estate Lawyer. Discuss what kind of Will or Trust you should have.

How much does it cost to set up?

Can changes be made at a later time? What is the fee for that?

WHAT'S NEXT?

You have learned an awful lot about yourself and your finances. Give yourself a hand for sticking to it and making life changes! This book aims to get you going, get you organized, and give you clarity in your situation. I can't stress the importance of this enough. You have done so much already, and you are probably wondering when do you get to the budgeting? Soon.

Part Three will walk you through making your own **Magical Budget Binder** and **Magical Future Binder**, which includes creating a budget and so much more. Don't be tempted to skip steps. Skipping steps can cause holes in your plan, and you might miss something crucial to setting yourself up for success. If and when your household's primary financial caretaker cannot communicate, you or your spouse or best friend or whoever can pick up your **Magical Budget Binder** and know when and how to pay the bills. They will have all the information for your accounts. I know that is a super grim thought, but it happens every day. You might even know someone who had a spouse or partner die or suddenly get hospitalized. While sitting in a hospital waiting room or grieving, bills are going unpaid, making this difficult time worse. I knew of a widowed woman who, instead of grieving, was playing detective to find where her husband kept their money. What a nightmare! And it happens all the time. Alternatively, you have saved the day by giving them the gift of security. Your family can properly care or grieve for you, knowing that the finances won't be circling the toilet. Rest assured that the work you are doing now is going to protect the family you love!

PART THREE: GETTING ORGANIZED

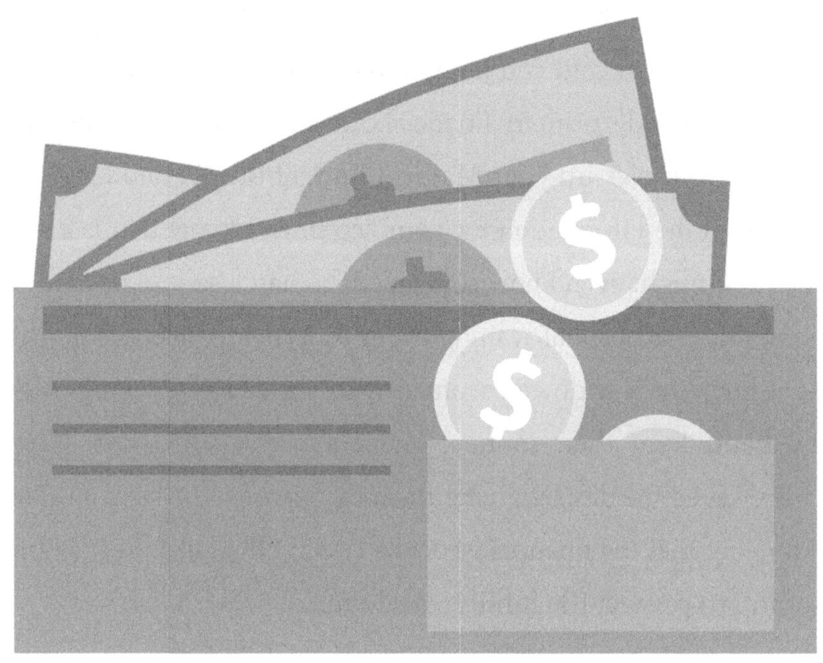

YOUR MAGICAL BUDGET BINDER

I hope that by now, you are entirely on board with getting your budget together. If not, do me a favor, agree to be diligent for six months, and see what changes happen. If you follow through and stick to your plan, you'll find the money you didn't know you had and feel a weight lift off your shoulders. Do we have a deal?

Getting Organized

OK, let's get you started!

First, you should have the supplies listed at the beginning of this book.

1. Keep a pen and highlighter on hand
2. Two 1.5-inch, three-ring binders
3. A total of ten tab, three-ring dividers
4. A pad of sticky notes
5. Extra paper

This workbook and your **two binders** are a set. You will label these binders: **Magical Budget Binder** and **Magical Future Binder**. With this set, you will overcome your doubts, create finance and life goals, and become your own finance hero.

Whenever we have a goal, we need a plan, and we have to track that plan. Whether it is a birthday party, a trip, or paying off debt and saving for emergencies, we must start with a plan, have a checklist, and stay on track. If the goal is out of sight, it is more challenging—some would say near impossible—to reach that goal. Your goals, dreams, and plans must be in full view for your brain to remember it, so our next exercises will go in your **Magical Budget Binder**, your "working binder," so you see them every time you work on your budget or pay any bills. These plans will help you pay off all of your debts, save a full emergency fund, and get you living your best life. I will walk you through all of this so you can take your life into your own hands.

A goal without a plan is just a wish. — Antoine de Saint-Exupéry

All of the worksheets you'll need for your **Magical Budget Binder** are in this book's index and at www.BestLifeFinanceCoach.com. Create a free login, and download customizable worksheets.

Arrange your **Magical Budget Binder** as follows:

On the front of the binder: **Debt & Savings Goals Thermometer**

Inside the binder: **Debt Payoff Worksheet** and **The Checklist.**

Now, you'll need the tab dividers. Take seven tabs and label them:

1. **THE PLAN!**
2. **Quick Reference**
3. **The Budget**
4. **Net Worth**
5. **Debt or Dream Life!**
6. **Mortgage & Taxes or Lease**
7. **The Bills: Utilities**

Next, take your **Magical Future Binder** and label the rest of the tabs as follows:

1. **Insurance**
2. **Retirement docs**
3. **Will or Trust**

These binders are divided for purely practical reasons. Your **Magical Budget Binder** is going to get a lot of use. Lugging around all your insurance and retirement documents doesn't make sense. You need these papers together and organized, so keep these binders together. Your **Magical Future Binder** is just as important, but it won't be getting much use once it is complete. As you get statements, replace the old ones from The Bills section, so everything is up to date.

As the years go by, and you fill up your **Magical Budget Binder,** file away the year-end statements for your records, and the rest can be shredded. Be sure to keep all the bills, insurance statements, investment account statements, and wills up to date. ***Getting organized is the first step to achieving financial freedom.***

Front of Binder: Debt & Savings Goals

If you have any debt at all, this is the time to reduce your expenses seriously, and then, as fast as you can, save enough to pay for a small emergency in cash. This amount should be **no less than $1,000.** A single car repair can be at least that much. Your goal is always to have **the cash to pay for unexpected expenses. Relying on credit cards is never a fallback plan.**

If you have savings **and** debt, set away some cash in an emergency fund and put the remainder of your savings toward paying off your debt. It made me very uncomfortable to pay off the two cars and deplete our savings, but it didn't hurt us. It lit a fire under us to save it back and more.

While paying off debt and saving your emergency fund, it is essential to ***cut all unnecessary expenses***. Eating out, monthly subscriptions, anything just because it is on sale. Even an annual zoo pass can cost you more than you think. Think about this a little more. It feels free because you paid for it (or put it on a credit card) months ago. But once you get there, you get lunch, or ice cream, or get the kids' faces painted, and the next thing you know, your "free day" cost more than $50. So, make a hard pass on the annual passes while you are getting out of debt. Take the kids to a park instead, or find local hikes, or the beach, or a lake and bring a picnic lunch. There are so many options for free entertainment. There are entire blogs dedicated to finding free fun. Anything that isn't keeping a roof over your head and your health intact is out!

Is it going to be uncomfortable? Yes. Will you want to get out of that situation as fast as you can? Yes. Will you be better off for it? YES!!! Cutting back isn't meant to make you miserable, but if you can't see past the immediate discomfort to the life that you are meant to be living, you'll never get there. Go back to the very beginning of this book and remember why money is important to you. This short-term sacrifice is for your family's security, to relieve stress, and so you can live a true, authentic, and best life. So yes, cut back everything non-essential to your basic living needs. The next section will help you make a plan for paying off your debts. The faster you pay off your debt and save your emergency fund, the sooner you can start living your life on your terms!

Tracking your progress is key to your success. If you can't see what is happening, chances of you getting discouraged, or giving up, is very high. Keep your goal right in front of you at all times! A copy of the "Debt & Savings Goals" sheet is in the Index on page 127. Make a copy and keep it on the front of your binder in the clear pocket.

The first thermometer will be the total of your non-mortgage debt. Include any student loans you have. People often want to ignore student loans, saying that it has such a low-interest rate that it doesn't make a difference. Remember that my car payments that were silently killing my dreams had a ZERO-percent interest rate. I thought I couldn't lose anything by having that loan. I paid my car off two years early, and two and a half years later, we saved enough for a down payment on an investment property. True story. I would have barely finished paying off our cars if I had kept going at the pace we were on. This investment has become a fantastic source of passive income that helped us catch up on our retirement savings. Our car debt was 100% holding us back from financial freedom, and we didn't even realize it. So yes, your very low student loan/car payment/personal loan keeps you from building wealth.

The second thermometer tracks how much you need to save for your emergency fund. The *minimum* amount to fully fund this emergency fund is three to six months of living expenses. For this example, monthly payments total $2,760. Notice that your income has nothing to do with this number. The lower your monthly expenses are, the less you will need to save for your emergency fund. When deciding how many months you need to save for, consider how long it would take you to get a new job. Some industries take longer than others to find new jobs. I was laid off a third time smack in the middle of The Great Recession, and it was taking some colleagues over a year to find a new job. I didn't start getting calls from recruiters again until over two years later. So, keep in mind the current job climate and your comfort level.

How to fill in your "Debt & Savings Goals" thermometer sheet:

1. Determine your total debt.
2. Add up your monthly expenses.
3. Decide how many months of savings you would like to have in an emergency.
4. Calculate how long it will take to pay off debt and save your emergency fund.

Then you will tackle your debt and savings in this order:

1. Save one month of expenses, no less than $1000.
2. Pay off all non-mortgage debts.
3. Save a minimum of three to six months' worth of expenses for an emergency.

Knowing how much you need to pay off and how much you need to save is the first step, and you already figured this out. Go back to the **Part Two: Outgoing** section where you added your monthly expenses, and the **Debt** section of your outstanding debts. These are your starting numbers. You will figure out how long it will take to pay off your debt in just a bit when you fill in your "Debt Payoff Worksheet."

If you are starting to feel anxious about this process, remember to breathe. Getting started is the hardest part, and you have already done so much work on this. Now, fill in the blanks and keep going!

Using the "Debt & Savings Goals" thermometer sheet to track progress

A: *One months of expenses = $___________________(not including what you save each month)*

B: *Number of months you want to have for an emergency fund:________________*

A x B = $____________________This is your emergency savings goal.

Total debt owed *(not including mortgage): $___________________*

In the example I will show you, I have arbitrarily picked $10,000 as the total non-mortgage debt owed.I have talked to people who have more than $100,000 of non-mortgage debt, so whether you have one thousand or one million dollars in debt, you will go through the same process. Write your total debt at the top of the debt thermometer on the "Debt & Savings Goals" page. Divide your total debt by ten, and write this number on the bottom "10%" line. In this example, $10,000 divided by ten is $1,000. Each line going up adds another $1,000.

The second thermometer is what you will need to save up to fund your emergency savings fully. Funding your emergency savings is going to happen in two steps. The first step is to save one month of living expenses, making sure that it is no less than $1000. For our example, the monthly costs are $2,760. This amount is how much money our imaginary person would need to pay for life every month. Once you have your one month of expenses saved, tackle your debt like your life depends on it! And it does, at least in the sense that this debt is keeping you from your real life, a life where your finances aren't causing you anxiety.

Take a look at the example here and start filling in your own "Debt & Savings Goals" worksheet from the Index. This page stays right in front of your binder, where you'll see it every day.

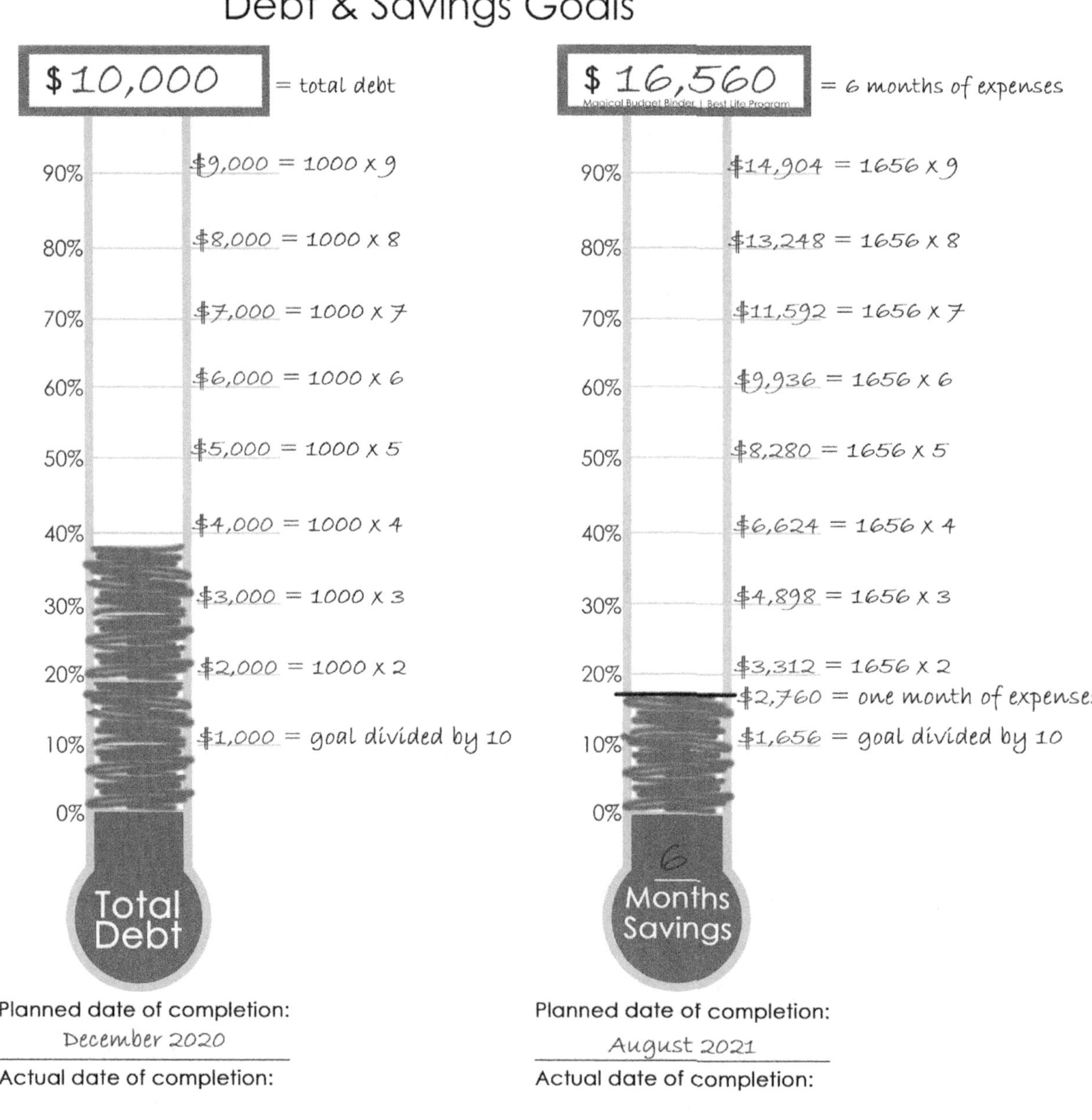

Pro tip: Once you have paid off your debt, take the amount you were putting toward debt, and put it toward your emergency savings. Once you have your emergency savings, start putting as much as you can toward your retirement.

Notice that there are spots to write-in dates for when you plan to pay off your debt, and for when you will have your emergency fund saved. Again, this has to be part of the plan, or you won't know if you are off track. I am going to show you how to calculate these dates next. Visually seeing your debt disappear and your savings grow motivates you. You will want to fill in your thermometer as fast as you can.I have heard many stories of people accelerating paying off debt once they have a plan, myself included. Our initial calculations had us paying off all non-mortgage debt in eighteen months. We finished in five months. How? We got creative, we buckled down, and we made it our top priority.

Plan for Paying Off Debt

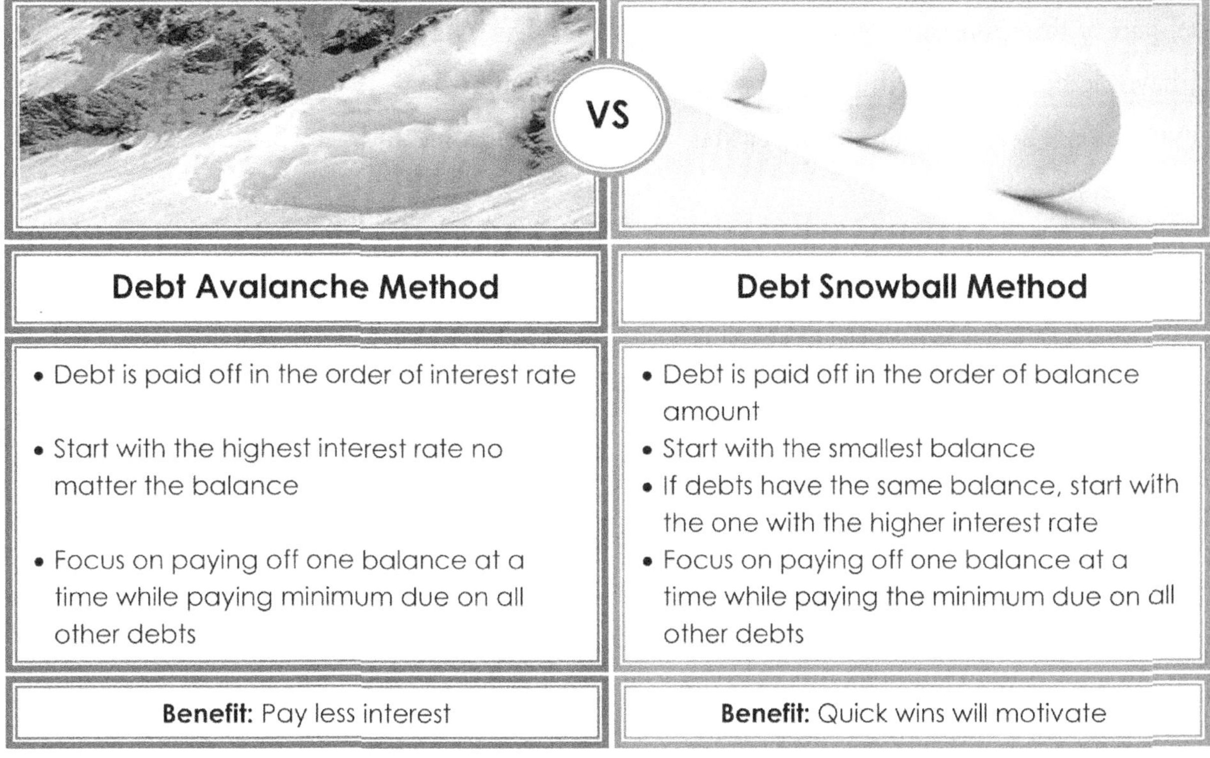

VS
Debt Avalanche Method
• Debt is paid off in the order of interest rate
• Start with the highest interest rate no matter the balance
• Focus on paying off one balance at a time while paying minimum due on all other debts
Benefit: Pay less interest
Debt Snowball Method
• Debt is paid off in the order of balance amount
• Start with the smallest balance
• If debts have the same balance, start with the one with the higher interest rate
• Focus on paying off one balance at a time while paying the minimum due on all other debts
Benefit: Quick wins will motivate

There are two main strategies for paying off debt. The Debt Avalanche method has you paying off the highest interest rate first. This strategy might save you some money in the long run if you can keep your pace up. The Debt Snowball method has you pay off the smallest balance first, and gets quick wins by building momentum. Are you motivated by quick wins or saving money? Understand which kind of person you are when deciding which method to use. Can you be focused enough to keep going even if you don't see a difference in the short run? Or do you need to see accounts paid off quickly to keep you motivated? Either way, get to work. Being free of debt is so liberating! And if you don't have debt,

CONGRATULATIONS!!! You are in the minority of people in this country, and you are well on your way to living the dream! Now is the time to focus on saving your emergency fund and ensuring you have enough going into your retirement fund.

What method did you decide to use? *Debt Avalanche or Snowball?*

____

____

____

Once you have decided on a method that works for you, getting your numbers organized is the next crucial part of this. You will need to find ways to pay off debt every way you can. Get side jobs, sell your stuff, have clothing swaps with friends instead of going shopping, make fudge for the holiday gifts instead of buying gifts. There is no limit to increasing your monthly income and decreasing your expenses if you are motivated.

Debt Payoff Worksheet:

1. Use the "Debt Payoff Worksheet" from the index and make a list of your debts in the order that you decided to pay them off.
2. Determine how much extra money you will dedicate each month to paying off your debt faster. You may adjust this amount after completing your Budget, but start thinking about creative ways to dedicate extra money to pay off debt. Write this dollar amount at the top of your page and fill in the worksheet with the **balance, interest rate** and the **minimum payment** amount for each debt.

Some of you might not be able to add much or even anything extra in the beginning. Don't be discouraged, the plan will still help you get ahead!

3. Add the **extra payment** to the **minimum payment** amount for the first debt on the list. Remember, you want to pay off the first debt as fast as you can, finding money from wherever you can to make this happen.

4. Once the first debt is paid off, add the total **new payment** from that debt to the **minimum payment** for the next debt on your list. The combined payment amount is now your **new payment** for this debt. Can you see the power of your money growing?
5. Fill in the rest of your table. You will continue rolling up your payments until all of your debts are paid in full.

Now let's find out how long it will take to achieve your goal. This will help you to always know the month and year that you will be debt-free and when you will have your emergency money saved! The longer it takes you, the more likely you are to have an emergency set you back, or lose steam, or both. I found this handy debt calculator that can be helpful. Try it out or one like it.

https://financialmentor.com/calculator/debt-snowball-calculator

If you don't use the online calculator, it will be harder to calculate how much your interest will be added to your debt each month, and your sheet may not be as accurate, but it is far better than not having any idea at all when you will pay off your debts. Once you have figured out how long it will take to pay off your debts, finish filling in your Debt & Savings Goals thermometer worksheet.

Here is an example of a "Debt Payoff" sheet. I used the Debt Snowball method and added $135 extra towards paying off debt. This worksheet is on page 128.

Debt Payoff Worksheet

How much more can you add to your monthly payment? $135 **Find all ways to increase your monthly payment**

Debt Name	Balance	Interest Rate	Minimum Payment	Added payment	New Payment	Notes	Pay more on month:	Original Payoff in Months	New Payoff in Months
Vet Bill	$468	0%	$105 +	$135 =	**$240**	*Cancel cable and reduce phone bill*	1	4	**2**
Visa	$462	24%	$116	$240	**$356**	*Added Vet payment*	3	4	**3**
Macys	$760	17%	$149	$356	**$505**	*Added Vet + Visa*	4	5	**3**
Home Depot	$1,350	21%	$145	$505	**$650**	*Added Vet + Visa + Macys*	4	10	**5**
Car Loan	$3,476	5%	$305	$650	**$955**	*Added Vet + Visa + Macys + Home Depot*	6	12	**7**
Student Loan	$3,484	3%	$184	$955	**$1,139**	*Added Vet + Visa + Macys + Home Depot + Car payment*	8	19 -	**9**
Totals	**$10,000**		**$1,004**			How many months **faster** will you be out of debt?			**11**

How long will it take to pay off all of your debt?____________(months & years)

What date will you be debt free? ___________

What will you do with the extra money after you have saved an emergency fund?

____

____

____

Your "Debt Payoff Worksheet" will be the very first page in your binder. It will be right in front of The Checklist until you are entirely out of debt. When you have paid off all of your debt, you can throw away, shred, or burn your Debt Worksheet while doing a happy dance, and vow to never take on unnecessary debt again.

Once you are debt-free (minus mortgages), save the rest of your emergency fund just as fast as you paid off your debts. Again, do this quickly so you can get on with your real life. If you only sort of half do it, and it takes you five years or ten years, your life is stagnant. **The longer you stay in this zone, the higher your chance of failure.** With your debt paid off, you only have essential monthly payments, and you should be able to do this quickly. So do it quickly!!

To review, follow this order:

1. Save for your starting emergency fund with one month's necessary expenses.
2. Pay off all non-mortgage debt.
3. Fully fund your emergency fund.

Then, calculate how much you need to be saving for retirement. You should be saving no less than 10-20% of your gross income. If you aren't contributing 20%, bump up your contributions little by little every few months.

4. Contribute to retirement automatically.
5. If you have kids, talk about college contributions.
6. Save for fun stuff! Live your best life! Be a fairy godmother!

The Checklist

I know I keep saying this, but keeping track of your progress is essential. Copy "The Checklist" on page 129 out for yourself and put it right behind your Debt Payoff Worksheet inside your Magical Budget Binder, before the tabs. Once you have paid all your debts, it will become the first page in your binder. The Checklist will help you stay on track—one foot in front of the other. Next thing you know, you will have your black belt in finance!

Tab 1: THE PLAN!

Nothing happens without a plan. The best intentions sit idly by without a plan.

Each year you will print out "The Plan!" sheet and put it behind THE PLAN! tab, keeping the most current year on top. Fill this out now, no matter what month of the year it is right now. Then, every end of December or the beginning of January, sit down with your accountability partner, review your previous year's plan, and decide what you want to accomplish this year. What would you like to change in your home, career, personal life, and family life? What are your savings goals, debt payoff goals, vacations, or new traditions or big purchases? Everything from repainting the bathroom to buying a new home gets put on the plan sheet every year. Your words, written or otherwise, are powerful, and when you set an intention on something, it gives it life. Write it down, and then do something immediately, anything, to get something on the list going. If it is a big trip, see how you can bump up your savings for travel. If it isa new job, start working on your resume. Some years you might get off track, and that is OK. Your path might change, and that is OK too. You still have a route you can get back on. The power of just havinga path to take is incredible. Your Plan gives you a direction, and then you just have to start walking. So, what are your dreams this year? Would you like to visit an elderly aunt? Or plant a garden? Maybe you want to get a puppy? Or save enough to buy a car with cash? Perhaps buy an investment property? Yes, that was on our list the year we did it. You can make it happen!

It takes as much energy to wish as it does to plan.
– Eleanor Roosevelt

Here is a sample page of "The Plan!" A blank "The Plan!" sheet is in the Index on page 130.

The Plan!

What are your goals this year? What would you love to do or see happen? Write it down! Fill in the blank lines with the category of your goal (Career, family, savings goals, etc.) and then what you would like to see happen.

Magical Budget Binder | Best Life Program

YEAR 2018 : "A goal without a plan is just a wish." — Antoine de Saint-Exupéry

Personal : Plan a family reunion for this spring.
Join yoga class.
Paint the bathroom before Thanksgiving.

Career : M - Talk to the boss about earning a promotion by June.
S- Get the Etsy shop up by February.
Enroll in woodworking class at community college.

Savings : Save Etsy money for travel
Open bank accounts for the kids.
Put $20 a paycheck away for home improvement

Investments Learn how E-Trade works. Set aside $50 from each paycheck to invest.

Travel : Yosemite, here we come!!!

Long Term Goals: Invest 3% more into retirement every year for the next 5 years.

Tab 2: Quick Reference

The Quick Reference section is going to be the smallest, but still very important. It is a list of your most commonly used bank account numbers, driver licenses, and frequent flyer numbers. Anything you need to look up often and don't want to hunt down. Why keep digging for information when you can have it at your fingertips! Having this list handy saves you time, and saving time can save you money! This list doesn't have to be fancy. Even a sheet of notebook paper is sufficient. Keep a running list, and keep it current! I have made a list of common accounts that you can print out and fill in for your convenience. It is in the Index on page 131 and 132.

Tab 3: The Budget (the heart of this book)

Before I get into a lot of numbers, let's understand why people have a hard time sticking to a budget, or even flat out refuse to try using a budget. People are emotional creatures, and managing finances is more about emotion than numbers. By going through the exercises in this book, you have uncovered a lot about your feelings revolving around money. If you need to review your answers in Part One, do so, and think mainly about what you feel when you make purchases, or how you feel when you have to pay bills. Remember why you are doing this. Does it seem impossible to feel freedom when it comes to your finances? I have seen countless people make their dreams come true. Your budget can make your dreams come true. Stick to it and put one foot in front of the other.

I am going to show you a few different ways to track your budget. I am a fan of having a detailed budget because you want to really understand your spending habits, know what you are saving, and plan for spending. A word of caution: Do not get lazy about your budget. ***If you are not planning where your money goes, you'll be wondering where it went.*** Your job will be to fill out a new budget every single month. You have already done most of this section's work, so look back at the pages under the The Numbers chapter. Start with one of the blank budget sheets provided for you in the Index. If the budget forms provided need tweaking to account for your life, cross out or add categories as needed. Write it in by hand for the first few months. Remember, you want these numbers in your brain! While you are refining your numbers, your budgeted numbers will need fine tuning, but generally, you can copy the Budgeted column over into the next month. After you have a handle on your budget and it's going along smoothly, go ahead and enter it into Excel or Google Docs or even Quicken, if that is your preferred method of tracking. It will save you time and make it easier to calculate changes. You will just be adding and subtracting, so take your filled-in pages and transfer your data onto your first month's budget sheet.

The first example of a budget I will show is a **Single Month Budget**. A Single Month Budget is the most common budget form you'll see, and I used it myself for many years. However, I have made one modification that we will talk about later.

The second example is a **Yearly Budget**, and as its name suggests, it will have your entire year's budget on one spreadsheet. It will take two full pages to capture your entire year. Each month has a dedicated column, and you can easily compare month to month at the end of the year.

The last example has a different approach to the forms I mentioned above. This is the **20-50-30 Budget**. While it looks similar to the other budgets, there are only three main categories: savings, needs, and wants. There will still be similar sub categories, but calculating your spending goals will be a little different. Both the **20-50-30 Single Month** and **20-50-30 Yearly** budget forms are in the Index and I will explain how it is different in a bit.

I am showing you these different options because, like with anything, people will gravitate toward or resist one method or another. The main focus here is to make a plan and stick to it. Over time, you may modify the way you are budgeting, or even scrap it and try another altogether. Wealthy people agree thata budget is key to success, so review these few methods and try the one or two that grab your attention. I will show you examples, and each budget will have a blank copy in the Index for you to copy and use.

Zero Budget

All the budget examples I am going to show you are "zero budget" based. The idea of a Zero Budget is that after you subtract all expenses, including what you are saving **after you get paid,** from your income, your sum is zero. If your 401(k) contributions or health insurance are deducted from your paycheck, do not put these amounts in your budget. Your budget uses only the money that you can physically use from your bank account.

A ZERO BUDGET MUST EQUAL ZERO. Whenever there is unexpected income, put it into a savings bucket or toward debt. Once you have paid off all your debt, the extra money will go to fund your emergency account fully. Once your emergency fund is set, and you are properly saving for big bills, decide with your accountability partner where to put the money. It might be travel savings or a home project or a new investment or a down payment for a house. The key is to have a plan for every single dollar. Whether you are spending or saving your dollars, you must have a plan for it.

My examples are based on a $60,000 per year salary. My imaginary person brings home $3,894 each month after taxes from their job, and an "extra" income of $450 from walking dogs each month, which varies from time to time. Some examples will have debts; some will be debt-free. Later, I will also compare the two scenarios, with and without debt. Before the month begins, fill in the "budgeted" column with what you expect to spend in each category. As soon as the month closes, tally up your real expenses from your bank statement and fill in the "spent" column. Completing the "spent" column is a crucial step! If you aren't accounting for where your money went, budgeting for it doesn't make much sense. If you estimate that you will need $300 for groceries, but in reality, you consistently spend $600, you are getting nowhere. ***Your financial situation will not change if you are not accounting for your spending correctly.*** And what happens if you habitually overestimate your expenses and you have extra money every month? Luckily, you'll have more options, but if you aren't accounting for it, you will not use it to boost your retirement fund or use the extra money as wisely as you could.

Irregular Income

If you bring home irregular income, you need to decide what numbers you will use for your budget. First, go back to your notes under The Numbers: Incoming. You wrote down the last six to twelve months of your income and calculated your average month's pay. Here are three methods to budgeting with irregular income, each with a pro and con.

1. Take the **average monthly pay** and create your budget with this amount. Use savings to cover low-income months and save when extra money as it comes in.
   Pro: No major pros to this method
   Con: Pulling from savings to pay for bills can add to your stress, especially if you have several low months in a row.
2. Use **last month's pay for next month**. Once you have at least one month of expenses saved, you can use the amount you were paid this month as your next month's income. For example, your July paychecks will go straight into savings. At the end of the month, you will create your August budget using July's income. You'll need to save a month's worth of expenses before using it to pay your bills.
   Pro: Knowing and using real numbers will keep you on top of your finances.
   Con: You will spend more time adjusting your budget monthly to account for the changein income.
3. Take the **smallest month's pay** and make sure that you can use it to pay for all of your bills. Use "extra" income to pay down debt, pad savings accounts, or invest with a predetermined plan.
   Pro: You will be saving like a champ!
   Con: No con! If you can live on your smallest paycheck, you are golden!

Creating Your First Budget

Starting your first budget can be overwhelming. Take one of the budget forms from the Index and fill it in with whatever you spent last month as a starting point. I will talk you through this process in just a bit. After you have filled in your numbers you will balance your budget so that it is "zero-balanced based." This will require you to add and subtract, and change numbers to make the bottom line equal zero. These numbers must reflect reality. If you zero out your cable bill but don't actually cancel it, this won't help you.

Even if your income covers all your expenses, cut down on unnecessary spending and call companies to see if you can reduce monthly bills. There is no need to waste money.

Then, calculate your category totals, marking down each percentage. Below is a basic guideline. If your percentages are different than what I have listed, take a look at the differences. Does it work for you, or do you see something that needs to change? For example, if you find that you are only saving 5%, and your rent or mortgage is 65%, work on balancing this as time goes on. Fine tune each month and find ways to make your budget balanced with your life.

Write in your percentages here:

Formula: monthly dollar amount spent per category divided by monthly income = 0.XXXX

Then, move decimal to the right two places to get the amount you are spending monthly in each category asa percentage.

Example: 440 *giving* / 4344 *income* = 0.1012... move decimal to the right 2 places = 10.12%

* All percentages are out of take-home pay.

Charity/Giving	$______/_______	Income =________	% (Goal 10-15%)
Saving	$______/_______	Income =________	% (Goal 10-20%)
Housing	$______/_______	Income =________	% (Goal 25-35%)
Utilities	$______/_______	Income =________	% (Goal 5-10%)
Food	$______/_______	Income =________	% (Goal 5-15%)
Clothing	$______/_______	Income =________	% (Goal 2-7%)
Transportation	$______/_______	Income =________	% (Goal 10-15%)
Recreation	$______/_______	Income =________	% (Goal 5-10%)
Medical/Health	$______/_______	Income =________	% (Goal 5-10%)
Insurance	$______/_______	Income =________	% (Goal 10-15%)
Personal	$______/_______	Income =________	% (Goal 5-10%)
Debts	$______/_______	Income =________	% (Goal 0%)

Single Month Budget

The Single Month Form is the most common example you will see out there. It is excellent for laying out your categories clearly, in an easy to follow format, and was my preferred method for many years. In this example, I have put a " * " next to bills that are often due once or twice a year. Each month, this amount will go straight into the Big Bills savings account to use when the payment is due. They might be different for you, so put your own stars or highlight the bills you pay a few times a year. Often, companies will offer discounts if you pay for a year upfront, so find out and plan for it—budget for these bills each month by dividing the total bill by twelve months. For instance, your car insurance is $1,200 for the year. If you have put $100 a month into your Big Bills account for your car insurance every month, you are all set! Simply transfer the money into your checking account and pay it. Total up these amounts, and every month automatically have this money transferred into your Big Bills savings account.

Earlier, I said that my budget forms were similar to what you will find anywhere with one modification. My versions of budget forms include your Savings Buckets and a withdrawal section to track when you spend from your buckets. As you save monthly for more significant payments or expenses, you'll want to keep track of the accounts that hold that money. If your bank doesn't have an option to send you a daily balance to your phone or email, log in and check your balances every few days so that you aren't caught off guard by low balances or overdrafts. By saving ahead of time, you add an additional security step in your life. There will be no more surprise bills or panic moments. When each large bill comes due, double-check your monthly amount due. Often payments will increase a little each year. By recalculating your monthly amount, you can easily adjust your budget before the next large bill is due.

What happens if you had been "borrowing" money from your Big Bills fund for little things here and there and your $1200 car insurance is due, and you only have $1100 in the account, and in two months, your home insurance is due for $910. Now you have a problem. Please do not be tempted to use your Big Bills money for anything except the bills you plan to pay. Remember, this money is already spent. It isn't yours anymore. Save yourself from anxiety and stress by leaving your Big Bills account untouched unless it is for a bill that is due.

Notice the savings bucket tracking area and note section in the example below. When you sit down for your monthly budget meeting, make notes on your actual budget. If you decide to make a change or you have an unexpected expense, write it down. Keeping notes will help you if, down the line, you can't remember why you pulled money from a savings account or why you decided to change your travel fund from $125 a month to $100.

Single Month Budget

MO/YR

Take home monthy pay	$ 3,894.00	$
Other Income	$ 450.00	$

	Budgeted	Spent
Savings (10-15%)	**Budgeted**	**Spent**
Emergency Fund (1st)	$200.00	$
Retirement Fund (2nd)	$200.00	$
College Fund (3rd)	$125.00	$
Housing (25-35%)	**Budgeted**	**Spent**
First Mortgage/Rent	$1,200.00	$
Utilities (5-10%)	**Budgeted**	**Spent**
Gas & Electric	$95.00	$
Water/Internet	$90.00	$
Cable/Streaming	$15.00	$
Phone/Mobile	$85.00	$
Food (5-15%)	**Budgeted**	**Spent**
Groceries	$325.00	$
Restaurants	$50.00	$
Clothing (2-7%)	**Budgeted**	**Spent**
Adults & Children	$100.00	$
Transportation (10-15%)	**Budgeted**	**Spent**
Gas	$185.00	$
* Repairs/Tires/Taxes/Lic.	$130.00	$
* Car Replacement	$100.00	$
Medical/Health (5-10%)	**Budgeted**	**Spent**
Medication/Vitamins	$60.00	$
* Doctor Bills	$100.00	$

	Budgeted	Spent
Insurance (10-15%)	**Budgeted**	**Spent**
* Life Insurance	$52.00	$
Health Insurance	$0.00	$
* Home/Renters Insurance	$75.00	$
* Auto Insurance	$100.00	$
* Disability Insurance	$65.00	$
* Identity Theft	$10.00	$
Personal (5-10%)	**Budgeted**	**Spent**
Child Care/Day Care	$180.00	$
Toiletries/Personal Care	$65.00	$
Gym/Subscriptions/Dues	$30.00	$
* Replace Furniture	$12.00	$
Music/Technology/**Misc.**	$40.00	$
Pocket Money (for adults)	$50.00	$
Charity (10-15%)	**Budgeted**	**Spent**
Thithes, Charity & Offerings	$220.00	$
Gifts (include holiday gifts)	$220.00	$
Recreation (5-10%)	**Budgeted**	**Spent**
Entertainment	$40.00	$
* Travel	$125.00	$
Debts (goal is 0%)	**Budgeted**	**Spent**
Car Loan/Credit Cards	$0.00	$
Total Income	$4,344.00	$
MINUS Category Totals	$4,344.00	$
EQUALS ZERO	$0.00	$

Savings Buckets	Withdrawal	Balance	Savings Buckets	Withdrawal	Balance
Emergency fund	$	$	Travel	$	$
Giving	$	$	Car Replacement	$	$
Big Bills	$	$	Other:	$	$

notes

Next, I will walk you through these steps that you'll repeat each month.

Every Month:

1. Download bank data.
2. Categorize each expense or credit.

3. Add totals and input in your budget.
4. Have a budget meeting and discuss progress, changes, and goals.

The easiest and fastest way to transfer your data from your bank account onto your monthly budget is by downloading the data and sorting it in a spreadsheet. Manually tracking your expenses can work for you, but it will take longer, and you may lose accuracy when entering numbers into a calculator. I am going to walk you through working your budget in Excel quickly. Apple Numbers, Google Sheets, or other spreadsheet programs will be similar. If you aren't super familiar with using a spreadsheet program, it isn't difficult. You just need to know what it can do so you can find where each button or option is in the program you are using. Ask someone to give you a quick tutorial of your spreadsheet program.

If you are a Quicken user, *go, you!* Download your data into Quicken and use this example as a guide.

If you don't have Quicken and wonder if you should buy it, don't think twice about it. I still use a simple spreadsheet for two reasons. One, it is easy, and two, it is free. Don't get locked into yearly or monthly subscriptions. If you can get the job done in a program that you buy once (or came for free on your computer), use that option. You don't need to pay for subscriptions year after year. Even a printed paper, pencil, and calculator will work for your purposes. It will just take more time.

Step 1: Download and align bank data

- From your bank website, download only the month you are reviewing into an **Excel or .CSV** file. You can choose a date range for download. Do not download a PDF view of your statement. .CSV is a raw data file that you can manipulate in your spreadsheet software.

Or something like this:

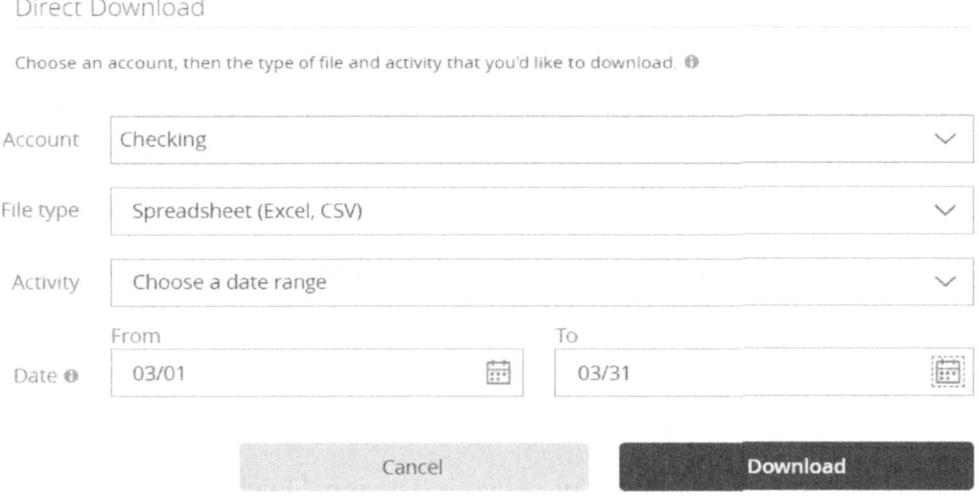

- Choose only the month you are working on and download.
- The file should open once downloaded, or it will be listed at the bottom of your screen.

It will look something like this example but with more detail in the description column.

Bank download 60k example - Microsoft Excel non-commerci...

	A	B	C	D	E	F	G
1	Details	Posting Date	Description	Amount	Type	Balance	Check or Slip #
2	DEBIT	3/1	ATM	(50.00)	DEBIT_CARD	459.04	
3	DEBIT	3/1	Gas	(42.56)	DEBIT_CARD	416.48	
4	CREDIT	3/1	Income from Job	1947.00	ACH_CREDIT	2363.48	
5	CREDIT	3/1	Venmo payment for dog walking	75.00	MISC_CREDIT	2438.48	
6	DEBIT	3/2	Auto Transer to Emergency Fund	(200.00)	TRNS	2238.48	
7	DEBIT	3/2	Gift	(59.45)	DEBIT_CARD	2179.03	
8	DEBIT	3/2	Putt Putt Golf	(25.00)	DEBIT_CARD	2154.03	
9	DEBIT	3/2	Rent	(1200.00)	DEBIT_CARD	954.03	
10	DEBIT	3/4	Vitamins	(10.00)	DEBIT_CARD	944.03	
11	DEBIT	3/5	Beauty Supply Shop	(59.84)	DEBIT_CARD	884.19	
12	DEBIT	3/5	Groceries	(89.43)	DEBIT_CARD	794.76	
13	DEBIT	3/6	Electricity	(50.00)	DEBIT_CARD	744.76	
14	DEBIT	3/6	Gas Bill	(45.00)	DEBIT_CARD	699.76	
15	DEBIT	3/6	Water Bill	(41.00)	DEBIT_CARD	658.76	
16	DEBIT	3/9	Auto Repair Shop	(398.00)	DEBIT_CARD	260.76	
17	DEBIT	3/9	Gas	(52.91)	DEBIT_CARD	207.85	
18	DEBIT	3/9	Gift	(38.98)	DEBIT_CARD	168.87	
19	DEBIT	3/9	Restaurant	(14.99)	DEBIT_CARD	153.88	
20	DEBIT	3/9	School Fundraiser	(25.00)	DEBIT_CARD	128.88	
21	CREDIT	3/9	Transfer FROM Big Bills to Checking	398.00	TRNS	526.88	
22	DEBIT	3/10	Gift	(17.00)	DEBIT_CARD	509.88	
23	DEBIT	3/10	Groceries	(75.41)	DEBIT_CARD	434.47	
24	DEBIT	3/10	Pet Insurance	(44.00)	ACH_DEBIT	390.47	
25	DEBIT	3/13	Clothing	(75.55)	DEBIT_CARD	314.92	
26	DEBIT	3/14	Medicine	(40.00)	DEBIT_CARD	274.92	
27	CREDIT	3/14	Transfer FROM Emergency to Checkir	400.00	TRNS	674.92	
28	DEBIT	3/15	ER Bill	(400.00)	DEBIT_CARD	274.92	
29	CREDIT	3/15	Income from Job	1947.00	ACH_CREDIT	2221.92	

Bank Activity | Step 2 | Step 3

Often the description will have large numbers and even location information. The description is whatever charge, transfer, or credit to your account so that you can identify the payment or credit. There will be times when a payment is unidentifiable at first glance. Try copying it and doing an internet search. If you really cannot figure out what the payment is for, there is usually a phone number you can call and talk to someone who can give you more information. There have been times when I have been legitimately overcharged, double-charged, or my card was used by someone else. By going through your charges each month, you'll catch anything that would otherwise slip through your fingers.

- If you also use a credit card or other banks, you can download them all, copy and paste the data into one spreadsheet before moving on to the next steps.

- Make sure that the Description and Amount categories from each download are in the same columns. You may need to cut and paste data into the correct column to achieve this.

- Double-check that the data you have downloaded is only the month that you need.

This document can look intimidating the first time you look at it. Don't worry. The only columns you really need are the **Description** and **Amount.** Ignore or even delete the other

columns. **Step Two: Add a new column and categorize each purchase or credit**

- Add a blank column next to the description.

- Type or write a category from your Monthly Budget Form next to each line item next to the description.

For example, if the description is the mini-golf place or movie theater you went to, write "entertainment" into the empty column; for a grocery store, type "groceries," etc. Use the categories you have on your budget to label the charges from your bank.

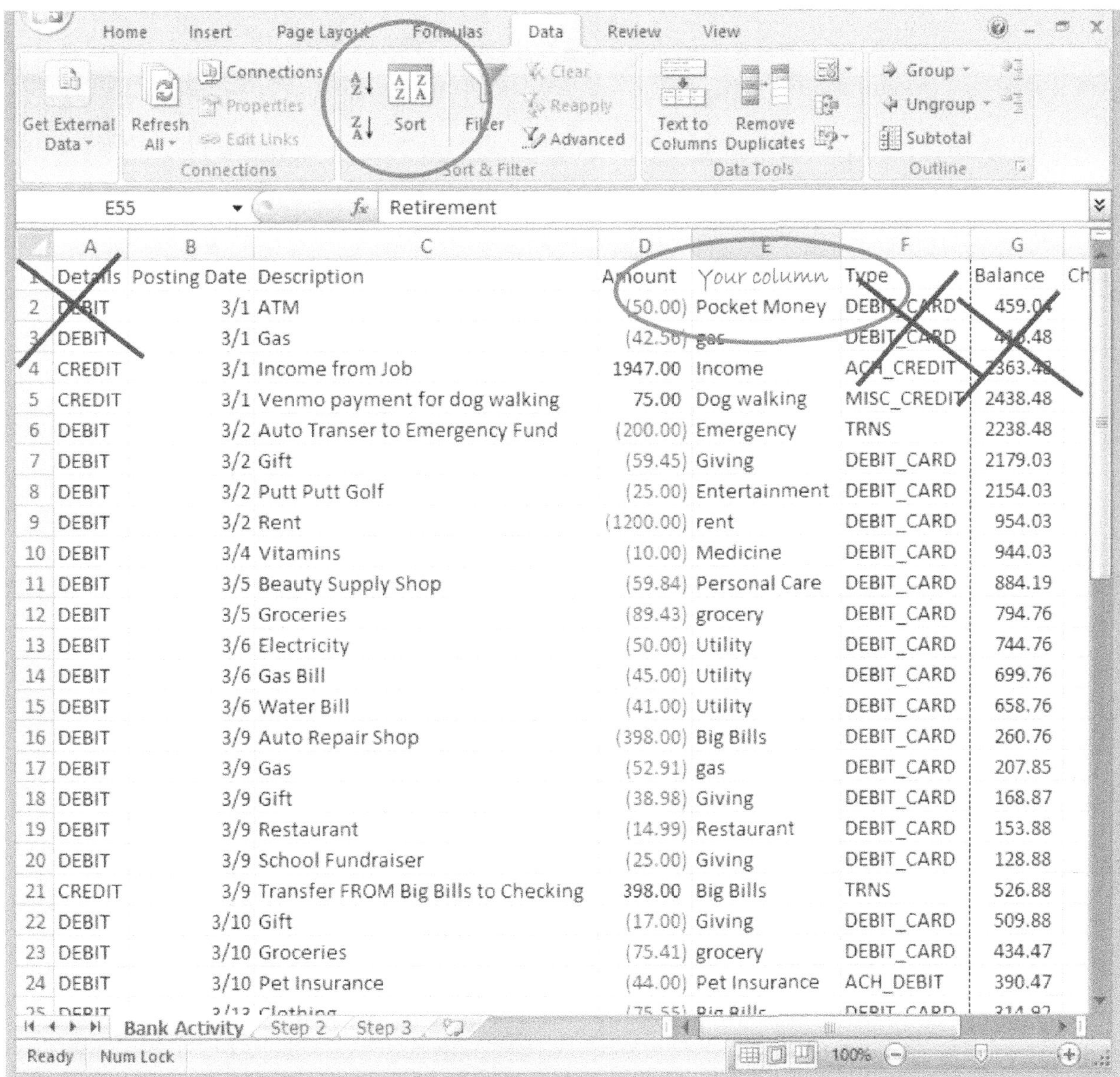

	A	B	C	D	E	F	G
1	Details	Posting Date	Description	Amount	Your column	Type	Balance
2	DEBIT	3/1	ATM	(50.00)	Pocket Money	DEBIT_CARD	459.04
3	DEBIT	3/1	Gas	(42.50)	gas	DEBIT_CARD	416.48
4	CREDIT	3/1	Income from Job	1947.00	Income	ACH_CREDIT	2363.48
5	CREDIT	3/1	Venmo payment for dog walking	75.00	Dog walking	MISC_CREDIT	2438.48
6	DEBIT	3/2	Auto Transer to Emergency Fund	(200.00)	Emergency	TRNS	2238.48
7	DEBIT	3/2	Gift	(59.45)	Giving	DEBIT_CARD	2179.03
8	DEBIT	3/2	Putt Putt Golf	(25.00)	Entertainment	DEBIT_CARD	2154.03
9	DEBIT	3/2	Rent	(1200.00)	rent	DEBIT_CARD	954.03
10	DEBIT	3/4	Vitamins	(10.00)	Medicine	DEBIT_CARD	944.03
11	DEBIT	3/5	Beauty Supply Shop	(59.84)	Personal Care	DEBIT_CARD	884.19
12	DEBIT	3/5	Groceries	(89.43)	grocery	DEBIT_CARD	794.76
13	DEBIT	3/6	Electricity	(50.00)	Utility	DEBIT_CARD	744.76
14	DEBIT	3/6	Gas Bill	(45.00)	Utility	DEBIT_CARD	699.76
15	DEBIT	3/6	Water Bill	(41.00)	Utility	DEBIT_CARD	658.76
16	DEBIT	3/9	Auto Repair Shop	(398.00)	Big Bills	DEBIT_CARD	260.76
17	DEBIT	3/9	Gas	(52.91)	gas	DEBIT_CARD	207.85
18	DEBIT	3/9	Gift	(38.98)	Giving	DEBIT_CARD	168.87
19	DEBIT	3/9	Restaurant	(14.99)	Restaurant	DEBIT_CARD	153.88
20	DEBIT	3/9	School Fundraiser	(25.00)	Giving	DEBIT_CARD	128.88
21	CREDIT	3/9	Transfer FROM Big Bills to Checking	398.00	Big Bills	TRNS	526.88
22	DEBIT	3/10	Gift	(17.00)	Giving	DEBIT_CARD	509.88
23	DEBIT	3/10	Groceries	(75.41)	grocery	DEBIT_CARD	434.47
24	DEBIT	3/10	Pet Insurance	(44.00)	Pet Insurance	ACH_DEBIT	390.47

Step Three: Sort and enter into your budget

- Once every line has a category type next to it, select your entire page and **sort** it by your categories. This step will group like purchases and credits and make it easier to get each category's total.
- Once you have sorted and grouped expenses, select all the dollar amounts for each category together. The total will be at the bottom of the spreadsheet. Put this total in your budget.
- Repeat this for each category. Here is the sorted example.

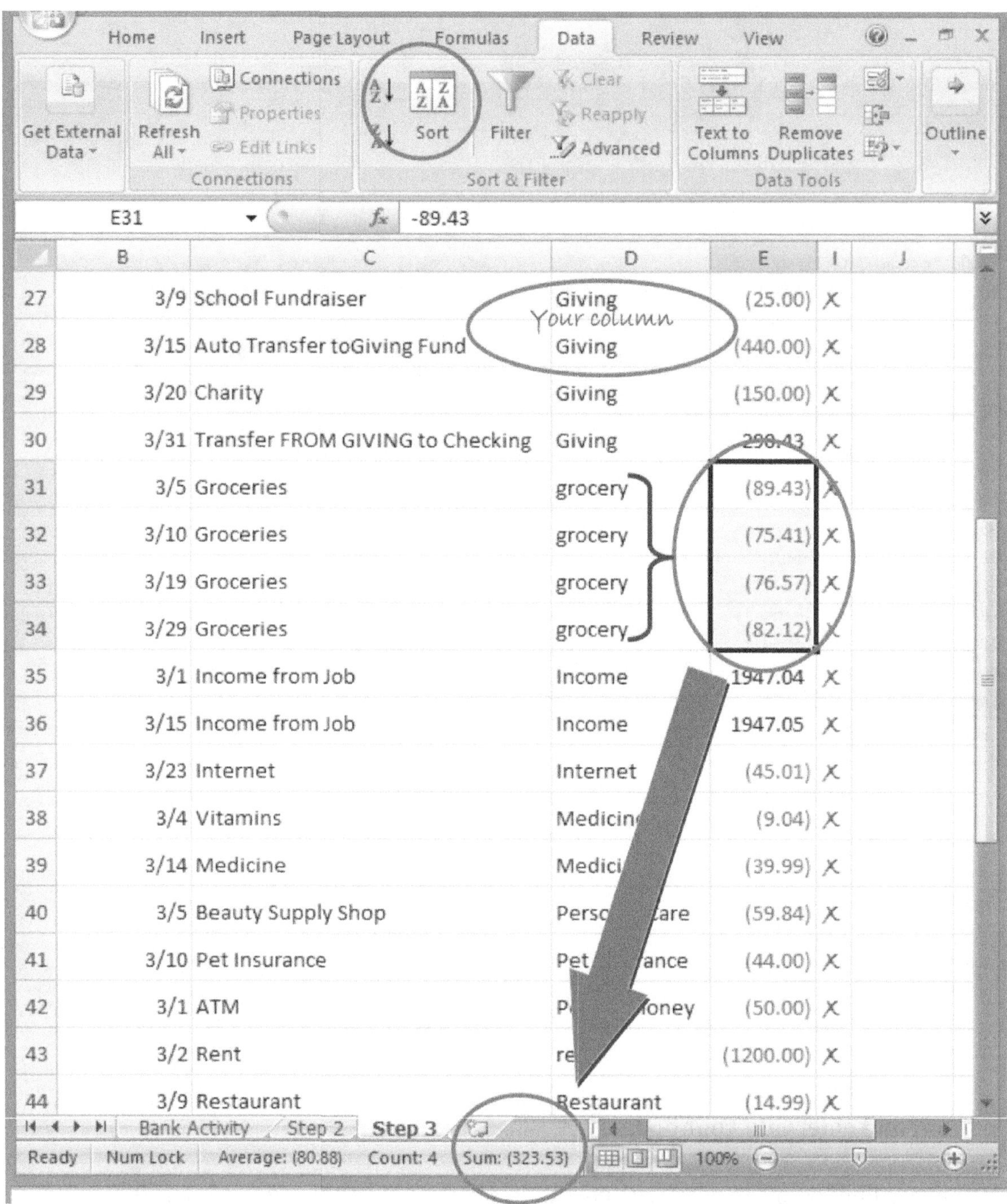

Notice I deleted the columns that are not needed. Even the date isn't mandatory, but I want to make sure no other month's data was downloaded by mistake. Selecting multiple dollar amounts at once will give you the sum at the bottom of the page. I mark each line with an "X" as I input it on the budget sheet.

After entering in what you spent that month, your budget will then look like this:

Single Month Budget

MO/YR: March 2020

	Budgeted	Spent
Take home monthy pay	$ 3,894.00	$ 3,894.09
Other Income	$ 450.00	$ 300.00

Savings (10-15%)	**Budgeted**	**Spent**
Emergency Fund (1st)	$200.00	$200.00
Retirement Fund (2nd)	$200.00	$200.00
College Fund (3rd)	$125.00	$125.00
Housing (25-35%)	**Budgeted**	**Spent**
First Mortgage/Rent	$1,200.00	$1,200.00
Utilities (5-10%)	**Budgeted**	**Spent**
Gas & Electric	$95.00	$98.20
Water/Internet	$90.00	$86.78
Cable/Streaming	$15.00	$14.99
Phone/Mobile	$85.00	$84.65
Food (5-15%)	**Budgeted**	**Spent**
Groceries	$325.00	$323.53
Restaurants	$50.00	$37.33
Clothing (2-7%)	**Budgeted**	**Spent**
* Adults & Children	$100.00	$100.00
Transportation (10-15%)	**Budgeted**	**Spent**
Gas	$185.00	$183.47
* Repairs/Tires/Taxes/Lic.	$130.00	$130.00
* Car Replacement	$100.00	$100.00
Medical/Health (5-10%)	**Budgeted**	**Spent**
Medication/Vitamins	$60.00	$49.03
* Doctor Bills	$100.00	$100.00

Insurance (10-15%)	**Budgeted**	**Spent**
* Life Insurance	$52.00	$52.00
Health Insurance	$0.00	$0.00
* Home/Renters Insurance	$75.00	$75.00
* Auto Insurance	$100.00	$100.00
* Disability Insurance	$65.00	$65.00
* Identity Theft	$10.00	$9.45
Personal (5-10%)	**Budgeted**	**Spent**
Child Care/Day Care	$180.00	$180.00
Toiletries/Personal Care	$65.00	$59.84
Gym/Subscriptions/Dues	$30.00	$10.00
* Replace Furniture	$12.00	$12.00
Music/Technology/**Misc**.	$40.00	$30.55
Pocket Money (for adults)	$50.00	$50.00
Charity (10-15%)	**Budgeted**	**Spent**
Thithes, Charity & Offerings	$220.00	$220.00
Gifts (include holiday gifts)	$220.00	$220.00
Recreation (5-10%)	**Budgeted**	**Spent**
Entertainment	$40.00	$24.88
* Travel	$125.00	$125.00
Debts (goal is 0%)	**Budgeted**	**Spent**
Car Loan/Credit Cards	$0.00	$0.00
Total Income	$4,344.00	$4,194.09
MINUS Category Totals	$4,344.00	$4,266.70
EQUALS ZERO	$0.00	-$72.61

Savings Buckets	**Withdrawal**	**Balance**
Emergency fund	$400.00	$16,107.68
Charity/Giving	$290.43	$1,426.72
Big Bills	$1,097.55	$2,641.85

Savings Buckets	**Withdrawal**	**Balance**
Travel	$566.53	$608.41
Car Replacement	$0.00	$1,967.85
Other:	$0.00	$90.45

notes

BIG BILLS: Car smog check, minor repairs and DMV fees = $398

Clothes = $75.55

Life Insurance = 624

Emergency - paid ER visit = $400

GIVING - birthday gifts = $115, Charity = $75, School fundraiser = $25, Walk for cure = $150

TRAVEL - long weekend by the lake, I reimbursed checking account with gas and food money spent

* Mrs. B cancelled dog walking service, new client to start April 6th

Remember how I said your budget MUST EQUAL ZERO? The budget plan came out to zero, but the actual number on this budget is negative $72.61!

Total Income	$4,344.00	$4,194.09
MINUS Category Totals	$4,344.00	$4,266.70
EQUALS ZERO	$0.00	-$72.61

What in the world happened? It was so well planned! Take a look at the income total. Less came in than was marked in the budgeted column. Now take a look at the notes.

notes

BIG BILLS: Car smog check, minor repairs and DMV fees = $398

Clothes = $75.55

Life Insurance = 624

Emergency - paid ER visit = $400

GIVING - birthday gifts = $115, Charity =$75, School fundraiser = $25, Walk for cure = $150

TRAVEL - long weekend by the lake, I reimbursed checking account with gas and food money spent

* Mrs. B cancelled dog walking service, new client to start April 6th

The notes state that one of the dog walking clients discontinued service, but a new client is ready to go April 6. Even the best-laid plans can go awry, and that is why we have savings! After looking at the notes, we can see that this month was actually pretty good! Our person had $150 less income and only negative $72. This budget has $40 built-in for miscellaneous spending that wasn't used this month. Chances are that this account has enough cushion to absorb that $72 without much thought. Notice there was a $400 ER visit and a vacation:

Savings Buckets	Withdrawal	Balance	Savings Buckets	Withdrawal	Balance
Emergency fund	$400.00	$16,107.68	Travel	$566.53	$608.41
Charity/Giving	$290.43	$1,426.72	Car Replacement	$0.00	$1,967.85
Big Bills	$1,097.55	$2,641.85	Other:	$0.00	$90.45

The Savings Buckets section of the budget is what you won't typically see on a traditional budget form. And it looks as though the emergency fund is fully funded with over $16,000 and the ER bill was paid stress-free! This budget has clearly done its job! Budgeting will do you a great service.

These savings buckets prepare you for significant expenses, giving, and other categories that need forethought. In the spent column, the amount budgeted for these categories will be transferred over to the savings account every month for later use. For example, this person will transfer $440 each month into the giving savings account. This month, our person only used $290.43. That is ok! This money is also for holiday gifts and charities. Likewise, $200 will be transferred automatically into the emergency fund. Even though $400 was used this month, it was there doing its job, keeping this person safe from financial stress and anxiety.

As you look over your budget and compare it with your initial plan, you'll learn a lot about how and where you use your money. You might realize that you need more money for groceries than you thought you did. Adjust this line item for the next month. Also, notice that the savings category is first. You need to pay yourself first before you begin spending your money each month. You might have different savings accounts than I have listed in the example. Make your budget match your life. If you have seven dogs, you might need a whole category for pet food, vet visits, and grooming. Customize your budget for you and your family.

Again, plan to set aside for bills paid yearly or bi-yearly. Keep in mind months that you tend to spend more money. Birthday months or holidays do not have to bring on stress if you have a plan in place. Once you have your emergency account fully funded and the Big Bills deposits are on auto, start in on your retirement account. If you haven't looked into what you need for retirement, go back to the Retirement section and calculate it. Lastly, startsaving for any college funds. Remember, we may want to pay for our kids' college, but not worrying about your care in your later years is a gift to them. Chances are, they would pick paying for their own schooling any day. Elderly parents without proper savings can be a considerable burden on adult children whomight have young families in their care.

If you are struggling to pay down debt, many of these categories will be a bare minimum until you have paid off all non-mortgage debt. Sure, if your shoes are worn through, get shoes, but be sensible. Buy bulk groceries where it makes sense but don't overbuy and have to throw out expired food. I asked a friend's grandmother what life was like during the Great Depression. She pursed her lips and said, "There are lots of ways to make oatmeal." I wanted to hug her and tell her she never had to eat oatmeal again! But hard times mean sacrifices. Having a fully funded emergency fund reduces the panic that comes from emergencies. Dave Ramsey is famous for saying that during the debt payoff phase of life, "you eat beans and rice!"

Copy several of the blank budget sheets from the Index and get going! Keep the most current month in front. I also encourage you to track your percentages for each category and make changes as necessary. Remember, this is going to take time to get right, but just the process of working this out over several months is going to help you in leaps and bounds.

Yearly Tracking Budget Sheet

The thing I love about a yearly tracking sheet is that you can see and compare months side-by-side quickly, and annual expenses and monthly averages can be calculated easily at the end of the year. These numbers will help as you set up your next year's budget. In this example, I have hidden several lines and month columns for the sake of space, but the numbers are still correct in the totals.

Yearly Budget

Year: 2020

	Budgeted	January	February	...	November	December	Yearly Total	Mo. Average
Take home monthy pay	3,894.00	3,894.00	3,894.00	3,894.00	3,894.00	3,894.00	46,728.00	3,894.00
Other Income	450.00	420.00	430.00	300.00	450.00	670.00	5,613.00	467.75
Savings Buckets								
* EMERGENCY Fund	200.00	200.00	200.00	200.00	200.00	200.00	2,400.00	200.00
* GIVING: Charity & Gifts	440.00	440.00	440.00	440.00	440.00	440.00	5,280.00	440.00
Investment/Retirement	200.00	200.00	200.00	200.00	200.00	200.00	2,400.00	200.00
College fund	125.00	125.00	125.00	125.00	125.00	125.00	1,500.00	125.00
* TRAVEL Fund	125.00	125.00	125.00	125.00	125.00	125.00	1,500.00	125.00
Car Replacement fund	100.00	100.00	100.00	100.00	100.00	100.00	1,200.00	100.00
Housing (25-35%)								
Food (5-15%)								
Groceries	325.00	301.00	285.00	323.53	409.00	338.00	3,719.53	309.96
Clothing (2-7%)								
* Family clothing + drycleaning	100.00	100.00	100.00	100.00	100.00	100.00	1,200.00	100.00
Transportation (10-15%)								
Gas	185.00	180.00	199.00	183.47	107.00	107.00	1,839.47	153.29
* Repairs/Tires/Lic/Taxes	109.00	109.00	109.00	109.00	109.00	109.00	1,308.00	109.00
Medical/Health (5-10%)								
Entertainment	40.00	36.00	45.00	25.00	45.00	35.00	465.00	38.75
Total Income	4,344.00	4,314.00	4,324.00	4,194.00	4,344.00	4,564.00	52,341.00	4,361.75
MINUS Category Totals	4,344.00	4,261.00	4,303.00	4,286.82	4,348.00	4,242.00	51,168.82	4,264.07
EQUALS ZERO	0.00	53.00	21.00	-92.82	-4.00	322.00	1,172.18	97.68
	Monthly Deposit							
BIG BILLS Withdrawal	**650.00**	780.00	1,095.00	1,022.00	1,967.00	679.00	6,768.00	564.00
GIVING Withdrawal	**440.00**	421.00	314.00	389.00	861.00	904.00	4,853.00	404.42
TRAVEL Withedrawal	**125.00**	0	0	567.00	0	938.00	1,505.00	125.42
EMERGENCY Withdrawal	**200.00**	0	0	400.00	0	0	1,306.43	108.87

notes

Jan - paid $780 for Disability insurance

Giving: $300 Go Fund Me, $75 school fundraiser, $46 gift for mom

Feb Big Bills - $910 for Renters insurance. Increase of $10/year, made adjustment to save $76/mo

Bought new shoes for M. and S. $185

GIVING: Foster kid fill a duffle bag project

....

Nov Big Bills - Car insurance due $1200, Car repairs $767

Giving: Christmas gifts and diabetes walk

Dec big bills: $188 fix car mirror, $183 clothing, $108 Identity insurance

Travel - fly home for holidays. Rent car.

Giving: Christmas gifts, womens shelter and help Tracy

Fill in the budget each month, just as the first example showed with downloading and categorizing expenses. Notice how the savings category is the same every month—saving with auto-transfers helps eliminate the temptation to cheat yourself if you fall behind in another area.

Look at the bottom of the page where it shows the monthly totals.

	Budgeted	January	February	...	November	December	Yearly Total	Mo. Average
Total Income	4,344.00	4,314.00	4,324.00	4,194.00	4,344.00	4,564.00	52,341.00	4,361.75
MINUS Category Totals	4,344.00	4,261.00	4,303.00	4,286.82	4,348.00	4,242.00	51,168.82	4,264.07
EQUALS ZERO	0.00	53.00	21.00	-92.82	-4.00	322.00	1,172.18	97.68

Notice the EQUALS ZERO line where there are months with positive balances, while others are negative. Again, this is because life is can't actually be planned out to the penny. The best news is that once the entire year is accounted for, you can quickly see what is working and what isn't working, making your next budget much more accurate. Remember, the longer you do this, the more comfortable you are and more accurate it gets.

See that even with some negative months, the overall monthly balance was positive by nearly $100! One reason is that the December income was much higher than expected. It looks like a lot of people needed their dogs walked over the holidays. Looking closer, you can see the monthly average for dog walking income was higher than expected.

	Budgeted	January	February	...	November	December	Yearly Total	Mo. Average
Take home monthy pay	3,894.00	3,894.00	3,894.00	3,894.00	3,894.00	3,894.00	46,728.00	3,894.00
Other Income	450.00	420.00	430.00	300.00	450.00	670.00	5,613.00	467.75

As you look at your numbers, make informed decisions about modifications to your budget. Maybe you don't want to count on the bump in business in December in case everyone stays home next year. You might decide to keep it as is, and if you do come into some extra income, put it toward one of your financial goals as a bonus. You might decide to use the dog walking money to only fund vacations and entertainment. Thomas Edison, American inventor and businessman said, "Opportunity is missed by most people because it is dressed in overalls and looks like work." Side hustles that pay for fun are great motivators and keep your paycheck paying the bills. Also, look at groceries and gas. Both of these were consistently under budget each month. Our person might look at these numbers and plan to use extra money differently next year.

The notes section for this budget form will be a running list on a separate page. You may need several pages for the year. Keep track by clearly writing the month or date every time you make a new note. Over time, you'll develop an instinct for what the numbers should be. Every month and every year that you are diligent will make your life that much more balanced.

20-50-30 Budget Form

If you can't stand the thought of calculating every category total, this might be a good option for you. In the 20-50-30 Budget method, you will have three main categories and fewer subcategories than the other budget forms. Keep careful notes, and you shouldn't have any trouble tracking your spending.

A 20-50-30 Budget can look like either of the methods I have shown you, but the one I am using for this example is similar to the Yearly Budget. Both versions will be in the Index for you. All budgets will start with downloading your bank statements and entering the amounts into the budget form.

Categories are as follows: Savings = 20% Needs = 50% Wants = 30%

Starting with the **Savings** category, calculate 20% of your take-home pay. The savings must go toward emergency funds, college funds, and supplementing other retirement accounts if needed. The 401(k) money that has been taken from your paycheck before you get it does not count toward your 20% savings. Having 20% of savings built into this budget is a massive plus for this system.

The **Needs** category consists of shelter, food, clothing, and transportation, and isn't to exceed 50% of your take-home pay. Keep in mind that your house payment should be 25-30% of your real take-home pay, leaving 20-25% for all your essentials, like utilities and car maintenance. If your home is significantly more than that, start brainstorming, this needs to change. In my example, I cut housing costs by giving my imaginary person a roommate; otherwise, I couldn't get the numbers to work. Car payments can quickly eat up large portions of this category, so paying for cars in full, buying used cars, and repairing vehicles over purchasing new ones will help you tremendously. If you are struggling to get by, remember, Netflix is a want, not a need, and every dollar helps.

The **Wants** category will be 30% of your income. Surprisingly, this is more than other methods allocate. So, my budget suddenly got a big boost in travel and entertainment! However, your budget must reflect reality, and as I found in creating the example, I ran into some issues. This category will include shopping, dining out, and any hobbies. As always, these are merely guidelines, so if your housing costs are high and your retirement savings are low, you may need to make adjustments and work toward balancing the numbers as you move forward. If you are still paying off debt, these bills come out of your Wants category. The faster you pay off your debts, the more fun stuff you get to do with your money!

The first thing you want to do with this budget is find out what your category totals should be. Take your total income and multiply it by the percentage allowed for that category. This will give you the amount that you will use as the category goal amount.

Savings Formula: *Monthly Income multiplied by 0.20 = Monthly Savings Amount*

Needs Formula: *Monthly Income multiplied by 0.50 = Monthly Needs Amount*

Wants Formula: *Monthly Income multiplied by 0.30 = Monthly Wants Amount*

In this example, the income will be the same as the previous examples, and I will point out some problem areas, including under budgeting.

20-50-30 Yearly Budget — Year: 2,020

	Budgeted	January	February	...	November	December	Yearly Total	Mo. Average
Take home monthy pay	3,894.00	3,894.00	3,894.00	3,894.00	3,894.00	3,894.00	46,728.00	3,894.00
Other Income	450.00	420.00	430.00	300.00	450.00	670.00	5,613.00	467.75
SAVINGS (20%=$868)								
EMERGENCY Fund	250.00	250.00	250.00	250.00	250.00	250.00	3,000.00	250.00
Investment/Retirement	400.00	400.00	400.00	400.00	400.00	400.00	4,800.00	400.00
College fund	218.00	218.00	218.00	218.00	218.00	218.00	2,616.00	218.00
NEEDS (50%= $2172)								
GIVING: Charity & Gifts	200.00	200.00	200.00	200.00	200.00	200.00	2,400.00	200.00
Mortgage/Rent	700.00	700.00	700.00	700.00	700.00	700.00	8,400.00	700.00
Taxes/HOA/Repairs/Furniture	20.00	20.00	20.00	20.00	20.00	20.00	240.00	20.00
Gas/Electric/Water/Trash	80.00	135.00	128.00	139.97	130.00	125.00	1,568.97	130.75
Cable/Internet/Streaming	37.00	67.08	67.08	67.08	67.08	67.08	804.96	67.08
Cell Phone	70.00	85.00	85.00	84.65	85.00	85.00	1,019.65	84.97
Groceries	315.00	301.00	285.00	323.53	409.00	338.00	3,719.53	309.96
WANTS (30%=$1304)								
Child Care/Support/Alimony	180.00	215.00	317.00	180.00	180.00	180.00	2,332.00	194.33
Personal/Pets/Shopping	90.00	276.00	208.00	259.00	255.00	214.00	2,981.00	248.42
Loans/Credit Cards	0.00	42.00	50.00	85.00	56.00	35.00	604.00	50.33
Total Income	4,344.00	4,314.00	4,324.00	4,194.00	4,344.00	4,564.00	52,341.00	4,361.75
MINUS Category Totals	4,344.00	4,636.08	4,699.08	4,681.70	4,650.08	4,480.08	55,262.58	4,605.22
EQUALS ZERO	0.00	-322.08	-375.08	-487.70	-306.08	83.92	-2,921.58	-243.47
BIG BILLS Withdrawal	**590.00**	780.00	1,095.00	1,022.00	1,967.00	679.00	6,768.00	564.00
GIVING Withdrawal	**200.00**	421.00	314.00	389.00	861.00	904.00	4,853.00	404.42
TRAVEL Withedrawal	**304.00**			567.00	0.00	938.00	1,505.00	125.42
EMERGENCY Withdrawal	**250.00**	100.00	405.00	400.00	150.00	200.00	2,655.00	221.25

Take note that the budgeted column came out to zero, and the income is the same as the other examples. However, none of the month's columns were equal to zero. In fact, they were almost all negative!

Looking closer, you can tell that this person is using emergency savings, and probably accumulating credit card debt. Neither is a good option. Notice how all of the utilities were estimated too low. Don't ignore problem areas. Fix them as they come up!

The Needs category should be about the same each month. I found with this budget that because the Savings and Wants category were higher here than in other methods, it forces the "Needs" to be less. Remember, I lowered the rent category by creating an imaginary roommate to offset house payments, but it isn't always that easy in real life. Again, this is a starting point and should not dictate your spending to a tee, but this is quite a consideration. If you decide to use the 20-50-30 Budget method, start with the 20% saving and add all your Needs. If your Wants category is sufficient, then you are fine. If you find that you are down to $50 left for Wants, then some profound changes need to be made, either to your Needs or how much income you are bringing in.

If you aren't sure which budget form to try first, pick one at random. Try it out for a few months. Then try another one. Starting is the only way to make life changes. Whatever reservations or fears that you have, shake them off. Budgeting is going to be good for you. All the budget forms are in the index starting on page 133 and on www.BestLifeFinanceCoach.com. Create a free login for access.

Envelope System

In the beginning, tracking your daily spending can be difficult if you are using debit cards. Consider using an envelope system. The Envelope System uses cash to curb extra or unnecessary expenditures. Once you have calculated how much you can spend in each category, take that amount out in cash, and only use it for these purchases. For instance, this budget has $325 allocated for groceries. At the beginning of the month, pull out enough cash to pay for your groceries. You can choose to pull out the entire $325 for the month, enough for half a month, or weekly. Now when you shop, you'll pay only the cash you have in this envelope. Keep a written balance on the envelope, so you know what you have left. This system works great for gas, entertainment, and other categories where tracking is crucial to staying on budget, and can be especially helpful if you have gotten into credit card debt. Studies have shown that using cash has a psychological effect on the brain. When a person uses real money, it triggers the brain's pain center while ***using credit cards activates the pleasure center of the brain. It is no wonder that credit card companies spend more than any other product company to advertise to us***.

With time and practice, staying in tune with your finances will become second nature. Small changes add up over time, and the accomplishments that you achieve will have no end!

Debt vs. No Debt

Some of you will still defend your debts with arguments such as they are necessary, or not that bad, or even unavoidable. Please keep in mind that the more debt you have, the bigger your liabilities are, and it increases your chances of a more significant emergency. Less debt equals less stress, the need for a smaller emergency fund, and, above all, freedom to live life on your terms. Below are two scenarios. Both examples have the same income and expenses, such as housing and utilities. The big, actually huge, difference between these two budgets is that one has debt while the other is debt-free. Please look and compare these two budgets and see what a difference having debt can make to a lifestyle.

What would you do with an extra $1000 every month?

Debt vs. No Debt Budget

	With Debt	Without Debt	
Take home monthy pay	$ 3,894.00	$ 3,894.00	
Other Income	$ 450.00	$ 450.00	
	With Debt	**Without Debt**	
Savings	Budgeted	Budgeted	
Emergency Fund (1st)	**$0.00**	**$200.00**	Zero Savings
Retirement Fund (2nd)	**$0.00**	**$200.00**	vs.
College Fund (3rd)	**$0.00**	**$125.00**	$525 Savings
Housing / Utilities / Food	same	same	
Clothes	**$40.00** →	**$100.00**	Yay! More clothes!
Transportation	same	same	
Car Replacement	**$0.00** →	**$100.00**	Saving to buy a
Medical/Health/Insurance	same	same	car with cash!
Pet Insurance	**$0.00** →	**$34.00**	
Personal	Budgeted	Budgeted	
Toiletries/Personal Care	**$20.00**	**$55.00**	
Gym	**$0.00**	**$10.00**	Can afford to get
Replace Furniture	**$0.00**	**$10.00**	a pet, join a gym
Pet Supplies	**$0.00**	**$20.00**	and have extra
Pocket Money (for adults)	**$20.00**	**$40.00**	spending money!
Music/Technology/**Misc.**	**$40.00**	**$50.00**	
Charity	same	same	
Recreation	Budgeted	Budgeted	
Entertainment	**$10.00**	**$40.00**	More fun, more
Vacation	**$25.00** →	**$125.00**	vacations and
Restaurants	**$0.00**	**$50.00**	eating out!
Debts (goal is 0%)	Budgeted	Budgeted	
Car Payments	$385.00	$0.00	
Visa, Macys, HomeDepot	$386.00	$0.00	Monthly payments
Student Loans	$134.00	$0.00	toward debts:
Other: Hospital Bill	$99.00	$0.00	$1004 vs. ZERO!
EQUALS ZERO	$0.00	$0.00	

What would your life look like debt-free? Who could you help if you weren't being held back with debt? Can you see how loans keep you from living your best life? Are you 100% on board with making and sticking to a budget?

Tab 4: Net Worth

If you haven't figured out your net worth, you aren't alone. The first time I calculated my net worth,I wasn't sure if it was good or not, but I had a baseline, so I kept tracking, and a crazy thing happened, it started going up! At first, it was just accounts I had forgotten to include, an old Roth, a 401(k) that my husband rolled over into a new company, some small, some not so small. Remember how worried I was about our retirement accounts? Well, I wasn't even keeping track of all of them, so yeah, I should have been worried! We were not paying attention! After I tracked down ALL the accounts, I still wasn't sure it was enough. It turns out that it wasn't and I never would have known that if I hadn't written everything down.

Locate the blank Net Worth worksheet in the Index on page 140, and just like The Plan, you'll see changes happen as you start tracking. This exercise helped us stick to our budget, because as we watched our net worth grow, we were more motivated than ever before. You will start making decisions that make more sense financially. If you have debt and few or no assets, don't be surprised if your net worth is a negative number! If you are in this category, don't despair, you aren't going to stay there. Remember, one foot in front of another.

There are two Net Worth worksheets on each page. Keep the most current net worth worksheet in front and make sure your net worth is increasing over time.

Here is an example of a simplified Net Worth worksheet:

Net Worth

MO/YR Dec 2018		MO/YR Dec 2019	
Assets: (What we own)		**Assets: (What we own)**	
Cash on hand	$1,000	Cash on hand	$1,000
Savings Act	$10,000	Savings Act	$13,000
Checking Act	$2,100	Checking Act	$1,800
Real Estate/Property: (Current Value)		**Real Estate/Property: (Current Value)**	
Home	$375,000	Home	$384,000
Investments: (Market Value)		**Investments: (Market Value)**	
Stocks/Bonds	$16,000	Stocks/Bonds	$19,000
IRA	$4,100	IRA	$6,000
401k	$241,000	401k	$276,000
Personal Property: (Present Value)		**Personal Property: (Present Value)**	
Automobile	$7,200	Automobile	$6,500
Jewelry	$2,400	Jewelry	$2,500
Total Assets	$658,800	**Total Assets**	$709,800
Liabilities / Current Debts: (What we owe)		**Liabilities / Current Debts: (What we owe)**	
Credit Cards	$600	Credit Cards	$0
Mortgages:		**Mortgages:**	
Home	$256,400	Home	$245,400
Loans:		**Loans:**	
Automobile	$3,800	Automobile	$0
Total Liabilities	$260,800	**Total Liabilities**	$245,400
Assets Minus Liabilities =		Assets Minus Liabilities =	
Net Worth	$398,000	**Net Worth**	$464,400

Notice how from one December to the next your Net Worth changes. The value of cars will generally go down while your home value will usually increase as the mortgage gets paid down. By tracking your Net Worth, two thoughts are happening in your brain. The first is to stop wasting your money, and the second is to find ways to increase your net worth faster! By understanding how your money is growing, you'll find ways to boost your gains. Nice job, you!

*What is your current Net Worth?*____________*Date calculated:*____________

The Bills

Next, you will be working on getting your bills into your binder. Keeping your accounts organized is key to helping your loved ones sort out your financial affairs if you suddenly cannot communicate with them. Whoever needs to should be able to pick up this binder and take care of everything! And guess what? You have already done some of this work! Use your budget as a checklist to make sure you have accounted for all of your bills. Be sure to add pages for anything that might not have a statement, like the location and key for any safes or safe deposit boxes.

These last several sections are going to need sticky notes. Put one sticky note on each statement in your binder. On it, write your login, password, pin, and any other information, such as security questions. Sticky notes might seem very low tech, and it is, because again, this isn't just for you, although it will also save you time and aggravation. The binder you are creating is for the grieving and distraught loved one sorting out your affairs. Whether you have left this earth or just left your abilities to communicate behind, someone needs all this information without thinking twice about it. Of course, while you are managing your own finances, this will help you out as well. Have you ever gotten a weird bill amount and thought, "I should check on that." But you forgot your password or what email address you used for that account, and it gets put off until forever, and then before you know it, that $59 double charge is lost to the wind. So, if you have a high phone bill, or if you need to cancel your cable (hint, hint), all your information will be at your fingertips. The rest of your monthly bills can be delivered by email or filed away, but keep one hard copy to make your life or your loved ones' life easier. Remember to update anything that changes. If you change your passwords or switch phone carriers, keep this part up to date!

Tab 5: DEBT or DREAM LIFE!

The first bills in your Magical Budget Binder will be any debt that you have—car loans, student loans, credit cards anything that you are working on paying off! Write on or put a sticky note on each statement with your login and password. If you haven't calculated your payoff date, now is the time to do it! Put a plan on each debt statement with extra payments and payoff date. If you are super organized, you can even use some sticky notes to create mini-tabs in this section.

Once you have completely paid off your debt, turn this section into your Dream Life planning section. *OMG!* You're going to love this! Vacation plans, hobbies, home renovation notes, whatever your dreams are will have a home in your Magical Budget Binder! You're going to make this happen! I am so excited for you already!

Tab 6: Mortgages & Taxes or Renters Lease

Yeah, these are getting pretty self-explanatory. Any mortgage statements or property tax statements, go here. After you have paid off your outstanding debts, you have a fully funded emergency fund and are on track with your retirement and college savings, calculate your payoff date for your home. Carrying a mortgage is one of those areas that you'll find differing opinions from finance experts. My personal preference is to pay mortgages off. Lowering your liabilities and bringing you peace-of-mind can be more valuable than using that money for investment strategies, which might make or lose money. Even once you have paid off your home, you still need to pay property taxes and maintenance, so keep that in mind when planning for retirement.

If you are renting, put your lease here. If you have a dispute or question for your landlord, you won't be hunting down your lease. Or, if someone else needs to get a hold of your landlord, it will be easy-peasy.

Tab 7: The Bills: Utilities

I think you are figuring all of this out! All phone bills, safe deposit boxes, streaming services, and anything you pay for needs to have a dedicated page with login and password and other essential information. Use those sticky notes and keep all this information up to date. If you want to be a real rock star, put your bills in the same order as listed on your budget sheet. You will be able to find what you are looking for faster and easier.

The **Magical Budget Binder** is your working binder. You will be using this throughout the month to pay bills, make notes, and stay on top of your budget. Being organized is more valuable than you can even imagine right now. Bills that used to overwhelm you will now have a managed place in your binder and part of **your plan!** This binder is going to propel you into the life you want!

MAGICAL FUTURE BINDER

So why has this been split into another binder? It is purely practical. Your insurance, retirement, and other documents can get to be a very large stack of paper, and you do not want to be lugging it around as you pay your bills. Once you have completed this binder, you will not be going through it very often, BUT, you absolutely need this information on hand, up to date, and ready for you or a loved one to pick up and deal with a big event. Keep this binder as a set with this workbook and your newly created **Magical Budget Binder.**

With your remaining three tab dividers, continue to fill in the sections as follows.

Tab 1: Insurance

If you need to review insurance policies, go back to **Part Two: Insurance.** Keep a copy of each policy in this section. Here is another handy place to use those sticky notes! A little tab between each policy will help keep everything straight for whoever needs it.

1. Life Insurance
2. Health Insurance
3. Homeowners Insurance
4. Car Insurance
5. Identity Insurance
6. Disability Insurance
7. Long-Term Care Insurance * once you are sixty years old
8. Umbrella Policy Insurance * once you have built up your wealth
9. Pet Insurance * if you have a pet

Tab 2: Retirement Documents

Your retirement documentation is so crucial to keep organized. With people changing jobs and rolling 401(k)s over into separate accounts, it is easy to lose track of where all your money is. So, print out a good old-fashioned paper statement and put it under this tab. And, hooray for sticky notes! Another great place to add simple dividers, logins, and passwords for each account.

Tab 3: Will and Trust

A Will or Trust can be a substantially large document, which is why you have a large binder to hold it. Do yourself a favor and put one of those sticky notes on the Declaration of Trust and Certification of Trust. Banks will want to see this page when you open bank accounts under the Trust, as all your accounts should be. Also, keep a note with the location of a copy of the entire document. Think about a close family member or friend who can keep the extra copy or a digital copy safe.

Are there more high-tech, less paper ways to have these documents? Absolutely. Can you scan everything and upload it to the cloud? Sure! But you have got to make sure that someone, or better yet, *several someones,* will know how to get to it quickly and easily. This Magical Budget Binder is Grandma Proof! So whatever way you modify this process, make sure it is easy for your family to follow.

Conclusion

This book is a starting point for you, not the end. You probably discovered feelings and habits that you didn't know you had. You might have uncovered reasons you got off on the wrong foot or felt inadequate in dealing with your finances. Maybe you were handed a financial burden that you didn't know how to fix. What you didn't know about money, or were told or not told about finances is not the story of your life; it is only a chapter. Your story changes right here. Your life needs will change, your circumstances, relationship status, your dreams will all change. And now you know how to create the ending you want!

As your net worth grows, you'll need to find ways to protect your assets. Talk to people who are further along the path than you. Read! There is no shortage of information out there. Most of all, dream. Do not settle for a life that keeps you struggling along. Break free from the thoughts that bind you into a mediocre life. Tell your brain how much you deserve it, believe it, and then live it. Today is the day you change your future, this is your time!

Before I leave you to conquer this on your own, I would like you to make a vow. By definition, a vow is a promise by which a person is bound to an act. Promise yourself, your family, and your future to be diligent in improving your financial well-being. And even if from time to time, you make a mistake or fall off track, forgive yourself and get back on it. Your dream life is entirely in your own hands, and you can do this. Make this vow now. After all, look at all you have accomplished already! Build security and wealth! There are many ways to be successful with your finances as long as you start and keep going. Talk to people about your struggles and accomplishments. Teach your kids all you have learned and encourage them to continue to learn. Watch your hopes and dreams become your reality. Be proud of yourself!

The Vow

I,__________________________[your name(s)], vow to continue to improve my/our financial situation by creating healthy spending and saving habits. I pledge to keep learning, improving, and growing in my/our life. I promise that setbacks, mistakes, or struggles will be taken as lessons learned and to continue the journey for true financial freedom.

*Signed*____*Date* ____________

*Signed*____*Date* ____________

Remember, it doesn't matter if you drop the ball if you pick it back up again. You've got this!

Congratulations, and welcome to your best life!

Shout out, and hugs and kisses to Adrian and Amelia,
who have supported and cheered me on with every
new adventure, every hurdle and milestone.
I love you with all my heart.
-DM

CERTIFICATE OF ACHEIVEMENT

proudly presented to

____

for completing the **Best Life Finance Workbook,** creating your **Magical Budget Binders,** and vowing to

____
Date

Diane Macias
Founder: Best Life Finance Coach

INDEX - BLANK WORKSHEETS

The following pages are blank for you to copy and use as many times as you need them or go to www.BestLifeFinanceCoach.com, create a free login, and download customizable worksheets.

Common Monthly Expenses

Magical Budget Binder | Best Life Finance Coach

SAVINGS

Emergency Fund	$
Retirement Fund	$
College Fund	$

HOUSING

First Mortgage/Rent	$
Second Mortgage	$
Association Dues	$
Real Estate Taxes	$
Repairs/Maintenance	$

UTILITIES

Gas	$
Electricity	$
Water	$
Trash	$
Phone/Mobile	$
Internet	$
Cable/Streaming Service	$

FOOD

Groceries	$
Restaurants	$

CLOTHING

Adults	$
Children	$
Dry Cleaning/Laundry	$

TRANSPORTATION

Gas	$
Repairs/Tires	$
License/Taxes	$
Car Replacement	$
Other	$

MEDICAL/HEALTH

Medication	$
Doctor Bills	$
Dentist	$
Optometrist	$
Vitamins	$
Other	$
Other	$

INSURANCE

Life Insurance	$
Health Insurance	$
Home/Renters Insurance	$
Auto Insurance	$
Disability Insurance	$
Identity Theft Insurance	$
Long-Term Care Insurance	$
Pet Insurance	$
Umbrella Insurance	$

PERSONAL

Child Care/Day Care	$
Child Support/Alimony	$
Toiletries/Personal Care	$
Education/Tuition	$
Books/Supplies	$
Gym	$
Subscriptions	$
Organization Dues	$
Gifts (including holidays)	$
Replace Furniture	$
Pocket Money	$
Baby Sitter	$
Pet Supplies	$
Music/Technology	$
Misc.	$

CHARITY & GIFTS

Tithes, Charity & Offerings	$
Gifts (include holiday gifts)	$

RECREATION

Entertainment	$
Vacation	$

DEBT

Car Payments	$
Credit Card	$
Credit Card	$
Credit Card	$
Student Loans	$
Other	$

TOTAL $

Debt & Savings Goals

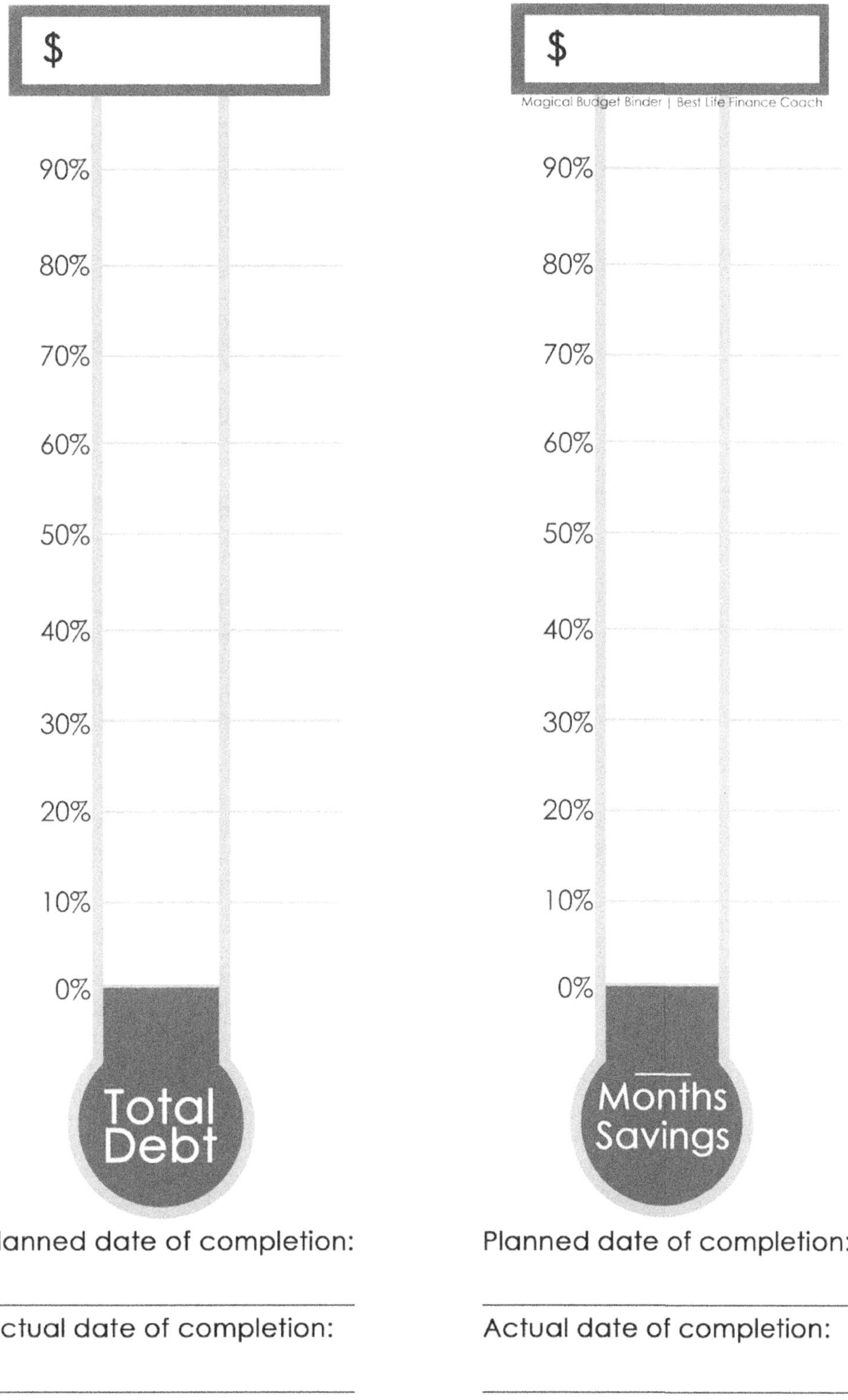

Planned date of completion: ______________________

Actual date of completion: ______________________

Planned date of completion: ______________________

Actual date of completion: ______________________

Debt Payoff Worksheet

Work Sheet Instructions

1 List your debts by **smallest to largest balance** or by **largest to smallest interest rate**

2 Pay as much as you can towards the first debt while only paying the minimum payment due on the rest of the balances

3 Once a debt is paid off, apply that payment towards the next debt payment on your list

How much more can you add to your monthly payment? [ ] *** Find all ways to increase your monthly payment**

Debt Name	Balance	Interest Rate	Minimum Payment	Added payment	**New Payment**	Notes	Pay more on month:	Original Payoff in Months	**New Payoff in Months**
Totals						How many months **faster** will you be out of debt?			

* * Estimates can vary due to rounding, late fees, or other charges.

Magical Budget Binder | Best Life Finance Coach

The Checklist

Magical Budget Binder | Best Life Finance Coach

1. Getting started:
    [ ] Identify and talk to your accountability partner.
    [ ] Complete your first budget and review it together.
    [ ] Set up recurring budget meetings at the beginning of every month.

2. Close the gaps - Cut back and earn more:
    [ ] Cut out all non-essential spending. ALL NON-ESSENTIAL SPENDING!
    [ ] Find a side hustle, ask for a raise, sell some collectibles, etc. to put towards paying off debts, and then to your savings

3. Save a month's worth of expenses:
    [ ] Whatever you spend in a month is your bare-bones emergency fund.

4. Learn to hate debt:
    [ ] Stop using credit cards irresponsibly. If you won't pay it off that day, don't use it.
    [ ] Decide which method you are going to use: Debt Snowball or Avalanche.
    [ ] Calculate how long it will take you to pay off all non-mortgage debt.

    I will be debt-free by ________________________ date.
    [ ] Share this date with people you love and trust to help keep you on your path.
    [ ] Post this date on where you can see it every day, and pay it off as fast as you can.

5. Save, save, save:
    [ ] Calculate how long it will take you to save a minimum of 3 months of expenses.

    I will have my emergency fund by ________________________ date.
    * Never stop contributing to your emergency fund.
    [ ] Review your insurance coverage. Do you have enough? Now that you have savings, look into reducing your monthly bill by increasing the deductible.
    [ ] Calculate your retirement needs and make adjustments where needed.
    [ ] If you have kids, decide what you will save for college.
    [ ] Start paying off or saving for a house.
    * Paying off your home early can save you many thousands of dollars, reduce your cost of living and bring you peace of mind.

6. Live your best life:
    [ ] Go back to your worksheets on what money means to you. Do something every day that gets you towards your goals.
    [ ] Be a fairy godmother to someone in need.

Quick Reference

Debts	Company, account number, login, password and contact information, notes
Car Loan	
Car Loan	
Credit Card	
Credit Card	
Credit Card	
Student Loans	
Bank Accounts	
Primary Bank	
Second Bank	
Business Account	
Retirement Account	
Retirement Account	
Investment Account	
Investment Account	
College Fund	
College Fund	
Housing	
First Mortgage or Lease	
Second Mortgage	
Association Dues	
Property Tax ID number	

Quick Reference

Utilities — **Company, account number, login, password and contact information, notes**

Gas Company

Electricity Company

Water Company

Trash Company

Phone/Mobile Company

Internet Company

Cable/Streaming Service

Cable/Streaming Service

Insurance

Life Insurance

Life Insurance

Health Insurance

Home/Renters Insurance

Auto Insurance

Disability Insurance

Identity Theft Insurance

Long-Term Care Insurance

Umbrella Policy

Home Safe key or code

Safe Deposit Box Location

Will or Trust

The Plan!

What are your goals this year? What would you love to do or see? Write it down! Fill in the blank lines with the category of your goal (Career, family, savings goals, etc.) and then what you would like to see happen. **Magical Budget Binder | Best Life Finance Coach**

YEAR __________: "A goal without a plan is just a wish." — Antoine de Saint-Exupéry

______________:

______________:

______________:

______________:

______________:

Long Term Goals:

Single Month Budget

Month/Year:

Take home monthy pay	$	$
Other Income	$	$

Savings (10-15%)	**Budgeted**	**Spent**
Emergency Fund (1st)	$	$
Retirement Fund (2nd)	$	$
College Fund (3rd)	$	$

Housing (25-35%)	**Budgeted**	**Spent**
First Mortgage/Rent	$	$
Second Mortgage	$	$
Real Estate Taxes	$	$
Repairs/Maintenance	$	$
Association Dues	$	$

Utilities (5-10%)	**Budgeted**	**Spent**
Gas	$	$
Electricity	$	$
Water	$	$
Trash	$	$
Internet	$	$
Cable/Streaming	$	$
Phone/Mobile	$	$

Food (5-15%)	**Budgeted**	**Spent**
Groceries	$	$
Restaurants	$	$

Clothing (2-7%)	**Budgeted**	**Spent**
Adults & Children	$	$
Cleaning/Laundry	$	$

Transportation (10-15%)	**Budgeted**	**Spent**
Gas	$	$
Repairs/Tires	$	$
License/Taxes	$	$
Car Replacement	$	$

Medical/Health (5-10%)	**Budgeted**	**Spent**
Medication/Vitamins	$	$
Doctor Bills	$	$
Dentist/Optometrist	$	$

Insurance (10-15%)	**Budgeted**	**Spent**
Life Insurance	$	$
Health Insurance	$	$
Home/Renters Insurance	$	$
Auto Insurance	$	$
Disability Insurance	$	$
Identity Theft	$	$
Long-Term Care	$	$
Pet Insurance	$	$

Personal (5-10%)	**Budgeted**	**Spent**
Child Care/Day Care	$	$
Child Support/Alimony	$	$
Toiletries/Personal Care	$	$
Education/Tuition/Books	$	$
Gym	$	$
Subscriptions/Dues	$	$
Replace Furniture	$	$
Baby Sitter	$	$
Pet Supplies	$	$
Pocket Money (for adults)	$	$
MISC.	$	$

Giving (10-15%)	**Budgeted**	**Spent**
Tithes, Charity & Offerings	$	$
Gifts (include holiday gifts)	$	$

Recreation (5-10%)	**Budgeted**	**Spent**
Entertainment	$	$
Vacation	$	$

Debts (goal is 0%)	**Budgeted**	**Spent**
Car Payments	$	$
Credit Card:	$	$
Credit Card:	$	$
Credit Card:	$	$
Student Loans	$	$
Other:	$	$

Magical Budget Binder | Best Life Finance Coach

Total Income	$	$
MINUS Category Totals	$	$
EQUALS ZERO	$	$

Savings Buckets	**Withdrawal**	**Balance**	**Savings Buckets**	**Withdrawal**	**Balance**
Emergency fund	$	$	Travel	$	$
Giving	$	$	Car Replacement	$	$
Big Bills	$	$	Other:	$	$

Year: ____________________ **Yearly Budget** Jan - July

	Budgeted	January	February	March	April	May	June	July
Monthly Take Home Pay								
Other Income								
Savings Buckets								
EMERGENCY Fund								
GIVING/Charity/Gifts								
RETIREMENT/Investing								
COLLEGE fund								
TRAVEL Fund								
CAR Replacement								
Housing (25-35%)								
Mortgage/Rent								
Real Estate Taxes/HOA Dues								
Utilities (5-10%)								
Gas/Electric/Water/Trash								
Cable/Internet								
Cell Phone								
Food (5-15%)								
Groceries								
Restaurants								
Clothing (2-7%)								
Family clothing + dry-cleaning								
Transportation (10-15%)								
Gas								
Repairs/Tires/Lic/Taxes								
Medical/Health (5-10%)								
Medication/Vitamins								
Doctor/Dentist/Optometrist								
Insurance (10-15%)								
Life/Health Insurance								
Home/Renters Insurance								
Auto Insurance								
Disability Insurance								
Identity Theft								
Long-Term Care								
Pet Insurance								
Personal (5-10%)								
Child Care/Support/Alimony								
Personal Care								
Education/Tuition/Books								
Gym/Subscriptions								
Pocket Money (for adults)								
Pet Supplies								
MISC.								
Recreation (5-10%)								
Entertainment								
Debts (goal is 0%)								
Loan/Credit Card/etc								
Total Income								
MINUS Category Totals								
EQUALS ZERO								

Magical Budget Binder | Best Life Finance Coach

BIG BILLS Withdrawal								
GIVING Withdrawal								
TRAVEL Withedrawal								
EMERGENCY Withdrawal								
Other:								

Year: ____________ Yearly Budget Aug - Dec + Totals

	Budgeted	August	September	October	November	December	Yearly Total	Mo. Average
Monthly Take Home Pay								
Other Income								
Savings Buckets								
EMERGENCY Fund								
GIVING: Charity & Gifts								
Investment/Retirement								
College fund								
TRAVEL Fund								
Car Replacement								
Housing (25-35%)								
Mortgage/Rent								
Real Estate Taxes/HOA Dues								
Utilities (5-10%)								
Gas/Electric/Water/Trash								
Cable/Internet								
Cell Phone								
Food (5-15%)								
Groceries								
Restaurants								
Clothing (2-7%)								
Family clothing + drycleaning								
Transportation (10-15%)								
Gas								
Repairs/Tires/Lic/Taxes								
Medical/Health (5-10%)								
Medication/Vitamins								
Doctor/Dentist/Optometrist								
Insurance (10-15%)								
Life/Health Insurance								
Home/Renters Insurance								
Auto Insurance								
Disability Insurance								
Identity Theft								
Long-Term Care								
Pet Insurance								
Personal (5-10%)								
Child Care/Support/Alimony								
Personal Care								
Education/Tuition/Books								
Gym/Subscriptions								
Pocket Money (for adults)								
Pet Supplies								
MISC.								
Recreation (5-10%)								
Entertainment								
Debts (goal is 0%)								
Loan/Credit Card/etc								
Total Income								
MINUS Category Totals								
EQUALS ZERO								

Magical Budget Binder | Best Life Finance Coach

BIG BILLS Withdrawal								
GIVING Withdrawal								
TRAVEL Withedrawal								
EMERGENCY Withdrawal								
Other:								

20-30-50 Monthly Budget

Month/Year:

Take home monthy pay	$	$
Other Income	$	$

SAVINGS = 20%	**Budgeted**	**Spent**
Emergency	$	$
Retirement	$	$
College Fund	$	$

NEEDS = 50%

Giving	**Budgeted**	**Spent**
Tithes / Charity / Gifts	$	$

Housing	**Budgeted**	**Spent**
First Mortgage/Rent	$	$
Taxes/Repairs/HOA	$	$

Utilities	**Budgeted**	**Spent**
Gas / Electric	$	$
Water / Trash	$	$
Internet/Cable/Streaming	$	$
Phone/Mobile	$	$

Food	**Budgeted**	**Spent**
Groceries	$	$
Restaurants	$	$

Clothing	**Budgeted**	**Spent**
Adults & Children	$	$
Cleaning/Laundry	$	$

Transportation	**Budgeted**	**Spent**
Gas	$	$
Repairs/Tires/Lic/Taxes	$	$
Car Replacement	$	$

Medical/Health	**Budgeted**	**Spent**
Medication/Vitamins	$	$
Dr/Dentist/Optometry	$	$

Insurance	**Budgeted**	**Spent**
Life / Health Insurance	$	$
Home/Renters Insurance	$	$
Auto Insurance	$	$
Disability Insurance	$	$
Identity Theft	$	$
Long-Term Care	$	$
Pet Insurance	$	$

Children		
Child Care/Babysitter	$	$
Child Support/Alimony	$	$

WANTS = 30%

Personal	**Budgeted**	**Spent**
Toiletries/Personal Care	$	$
Education/Tuition/Books	$	$
Gym/Subscriptions/Dues	$	$
Replace Furniture	$	$
Pet Supplies	$	$
Pocket Money (for adults)	$	$
MISC.	$	$

Recreation	**Budgeted**	**Spent**
Entertainment	$	$
Travel		

Debts (goal is zero)	**Budgeted**	**Spent**
Car Payments	$	$
Credit Card:	$	$
Credit Card:	$	$
Credit Card:	$	$
Student Loans	$	$
Other:	$	$

Magical Budget Binder | Best Life Finance Coach

Total Income	$	$
MINUS Category Totals	$	$
EQUALS ZERO	$	$

Savings Buckets	**Withdrawal**	**Balance**
Emergency fund	$	$
Giving	$	$
Big Bills	$	$

Savings Buckets	**Withdrawal**	**Balance**
Travel	$	$
Car Replacement	$	$
Other:	$	$

notes

Budget Notes

Year:

20-30-50 Yearly Budget

Jan - July

	Budgeted	January	February	March	April	May	June	July
Monthly Take Home Pay								
Other Income								
SAVINGS 20% =								
Emergency								
Retirement/College								
NEEDS 50% =								
Giving								
Tithes, Charity & Gifts								
Housing								
Mortgage/Rent/Taxes/HOA								
Maintenance/Other								
Utilities								
Gas/Electric								
Water/Trash								
Cable/Internet								
Cell Phone								
Food								
Groceries								
Restaurants								
Clothing								
Family clothing + dry-cleaning								
Transportation								
Gas								
Repairs/Tires/Lic/Taxes								
Car Replacement								
Medical/Health								
Medication/Bills								
Insurance								
Life Insurance/Health								
Home/Renters/Auto								
Disability/Identity								
Child Care/Support/Alimony								
WANTS 30% =								
Personal								
Personal Care								
Education/Tuition/Books								
Gym/Subscriptions								
Pocket Money (for adults)								
Pet Supplies								
MISC.								
Recreation								
Entertainment								
Travel								
Debts (goal is 0%)								
Debts:								
Total Income								
MINUS Category Totals								
EQUALS ZERO								

Magical Budget Binder | Best Life Finance Coach

	Budgeted	January	February	March	April	May	June	July
BIG BILLS Withdrawal								
GIVING Withdrawal								
TRAVEL Withdrawal								
EMERGENCY Withdrawal								
Other:								

Year:

20-30-50 Yearly Budget

Aug - Dec + Totals

	Budgeted	August	September	October	November	December	Yearly Total	Average
Monthly Take Home Pay								
Other Income								
SAVINGS 20% =								
Emergency								
Retirement/College								
NEEDS 50% =								
Giving								
Tithes, Charity & Gifts								
Housing								
Mortgage/Rent/Taxes/HOA								
Maintenance/Other								
Utilities								
Gas/Electric								
Water/Trash								
Cable/Internet								
Cell Phone								
Food								
Groceries								
Restaurants								
Clothing								
Family clothing + dry-cleaning								
Transportation								
Gas								
Repairs/Tires/Lic/Taxes								
Car Replacement								
Medical/Health								
Medication/Bills								
Insurance								
Life Insurance/Health								
Home/Renters/Auto								
Disability/Identity								
Child Care/Support/Alimony								
WANTS 30% =								
Personal								
Personal Care								
Education/Tuition/Books								
Gym/Subscriptions								
Pocket Money (for adults)								
Pet Supplies								
MISC.								
Recreation								
Entertainment								
Travel								
Debts (goal is 0%)								
Debts:								
Total Income								
MINUS Category Totals								
EQUALS ZERO								

Magical Budget Binder | Best Life Finance Coach

BIG BILLS Withdrawal								
GIVING Withdrawal								
TRAVEL Withdrawal								
EMERGENCY Withdrawal								
Other:								

Net Worth

Calculate Net Worth4x per year

MO/YR		**MO/YR**	
Assets: (What we own)		**Assets: (What we own)**	
Cash on hand	$	Cash on hand	$
Savings Act	$	Savings Act	$
Checking Act	$	Checking Act	$
Cash value of life Insur.	$	Cash value of life Insur.	$
Real Estate/Property: (Current Value)		**Real Estate/Property: (Current Value)**	
Home	$	Home	$
Land	$	Land	$
Investments: (Market Value)		**Investments: (Market Value)**	
Certificate of Deposit	$	Certificate of Deposit	$
Stocks/Bonds	$	Stocks/Bonds	$
Mutual Funds	$	Mutual Funds	$
Annuities	$	Annuities	$
IRA	$	IRA	$
401k	$	401k	$
Pension	$	Pension	$
Other	$	Other	$
Personal Property: (Present Value)		**Personal Property: (Present Value)**	
Automobile	$	Automobile	$
Recreational Vehicle	$	Recreational Vehicle	$
Jewelry	$	Jewelry	$
Home furninshings	$	Home furninshings	$
Appliances & Furniture	$	Appliances & Furniture	$
Collections	$	Collections	$
Total Assets		**Total Assets**	
Liabilities (What we owe)		**Liabilities (What we owe)**	
Current Debts:		**Current Debts:**	
Medical	$	Medical	$
Credit Cards	$	Credit Cards	$
Legal/Taxes	$	Legal/Taxes	$
Mortgages:		**Mortgages:**	
Home	$	Home	$
Land	$	Land	$
Loans:		**Loans:**	
Automobile	$	Automobile	$
Personal	$	Personal	$
Education	$	Education	$
Bank/Finance	$	Bank/Finance	$
Total Liabilities		**Total Liabilities**	
Assets Minus Liabilities =		Assets Minus Liabilities =	
Net Worth		**Net Worth**	

Kids $1000 Emergency Fund

How it works:
Each block represents $25. As you save, color the blocks in and keep track of your progress!
Your goal is to have $1000 by the time you are $18!

- How many years do you have before you turn 18?
- How many months is that?
- How much do you need to save each month to make it?
- How much more would you like to have?

START

$50

Oooh My GOSH!!
You're off to such a good start!

$250

$150

YOU ARE AMAZING!!
You know that, right?

$500

$300

$425

DON'T GIVE UP!
You're crushing this!

$650

$750

$900

FINISH

Want a boost?

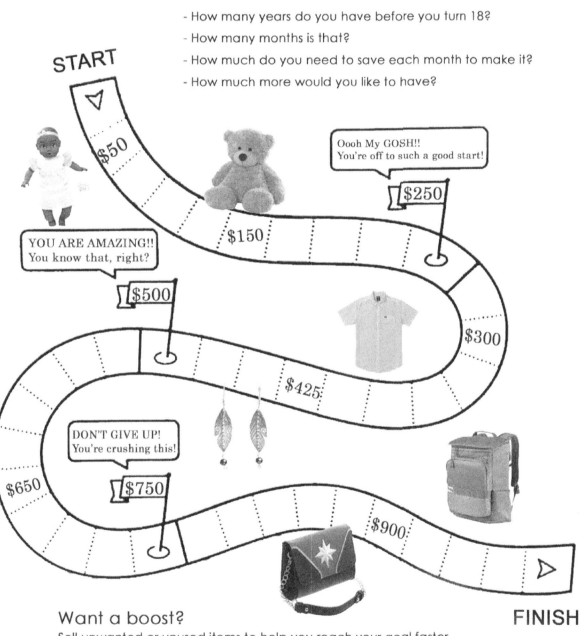

Sell unwanted or unused items to help you reach your goal faster.
Askk people what jobs you can help them with for some extra money!

Name: Age: Start Date:

Made in the USA
Columbia, SC
12 April 2024